To my grandmother, Florence
who took me on my first tr

and

To Terry, John, and Le
who took me on my second

Great American Rail Journeys

THE COMPANION

TO THE PUBLIC

TELEVISION

JOHN GRANT

PROGRAMS

The
Globe
Pequot
Press

Guilford, Connecticut

Cover and page design by Bill Brown
Layout and production by Deborah Nicolais
Cover photo by Matthew G. Wheeler
Maps by MaryAnn Dubé
Photo credits: p. iii: Brian Solomon; p. viii: Calvin W. Hall
Randy Brandon/Third Eye Photography; pp. 26–27: Brian
48–49: ©Kerrick James; pp. 72–73: American Orient Expr
Carl and Ann Purcell; pp. 96–97: Matthew G. Wheeler; pp
©Amtrak; pp. 142–43: ©Amtrak; pp. 166–67: John Gran
credits appear with photos.

Library of Congress Cataloging-in-Publication Data
Grant, John, 1948–
    Great American rail journeys : the companion to the pu
    programs / John Grant.—1st ed.
        p. cm.
    Includes index.
    ISBN 0-7627-0738-0 (hardcover)—ISBN 0-7627-0614
    1. United States—Description and travel. 2. Unites St
works. 3. Railroad travel—United States. 4. Railroad tr
States—Pictorial works. I. Title.

E169.04.G735 2000
917.304'929—dc21

First Edition / First Printing
Printed in Canada

Great American Rail Journeys

THE COMPANION

TO THE PUBLIC

TELEVISION

JOHN GRANT

PROGRAMS

The Globe Pequot Press

Guilford, Connecticut

Cover and page design by Bill Brown
Layout and production by Deborah Nicolais
Cover photo by Matthew G. Wheeler
Maps by MaryAnn Dubé
Photo credits: p. iii: Brian Solomon; p. viii: Calvin W. Hall; pp. 2–3: Randy Brandon/Third Eye Photography; pp. 26–27: Brian Solomon; pp. 48–49: ©Kerrick James; pp. 72–73: American Orient Express Photo by Carl and Ann Purcell; pp. 96–97: Matthew G. Wheeler; pp. 118–19: ©Amtrak; pp. 142–43: ©Amtrak; pp. 166–67: John Grant. All other credits appear with photos.

Library of Congress Cataloging-in-Publication Data
Grant, John, 1948–
   Great American rail journeys : the companion to the public television programs / John Grant.—1st ed.
     p. cm.
  Includes index.
  ISBN 0-7627-0738-0 (hardcover)—ISBN 0-7627-0614-7 (pbk.)
  1. United States—Description and travel. 2. Unites States—Pictorial works. 3. Railroad travel—United States. 4. Railroad travel—United States—Pictorial works. I. Title.

E169.04.G735 2000
917.304'929—dc21

00-037179

First Edition / First Printing
Printed in Canada

To my grandmother, Florence Dobson,
who took me on my first train trip

and

To Terry, John, and Lee,
who took me on my second train trip

Contents

Acknowledgments

If you're ever hung around for the closing credits of a television program you have some idea of how many people it takes to make one of the train documentaries we've done for public television. Many talented cameramen, audio specialists, editors, producers, directors, and writers helped create the television programs that were the foundation for the stories in *Great American Rail Journeys*. This book would not be possible without the quality work of those dedicated television professionals.

Television programs don't get made without funding. Pat Faust, then vice president of the American Program Service, funded the first series of six train programs called *America's Scenic Rail Journeys*. I will always be grateful to Pat for her confidence and early support of Driftwood Productions. PBS has provided funding for the most recent train specials, and I want to thank John Wilson, Steven Gray, and Mary Jane McKinven for their continued support and interest in this genre of programming.

The coproduction partner for all of the train programs is Oregon Public Broadcasting. I want to thank Maynard Orme (a devoted rail fan), Debbi Hinton, and John Lindsay at OPB for their continued support. Many others at OPB also made significant contributions to these programs, most especially John Booth. Acorn Media Publishing in Bethesda, Maryland, is also a partner on the train programs. Peter Edwards and John Lorenz provided needed funding, enthusiastic support, and critical advice when it was most needed.

Hundreds of railroad personnel, some of them mentioned in the pages of this book, contributed to the making of the television programs and the book. Although they are too numerous to mention here, we are grateful for the extra assistance provided by the countless Amtrak conductors, VIA Rail engineers, AOE staff, and many others. Two people in particular typify the uniformly enthusiastic assistance we received—Bill Pickeral of the *Sierra Madre Express* and Tina Cyr of the *White Pass & Yukon Route Railroad*. Both seem to have way too much fun doing their jobs.

I've often joked with friends that writing 50,000 words isn't all that difficult, it's getting the words in the right order that is the challenge. To the degree that most of the words in this book are in the right order, I am grateful to Laura Strom, the executive editor at Globe Pequot Press, and Doe Boyle, the editor of the manuscript. Laura has been an enthusiastic supporter of the book and a valuable source of encouragement. Doe's careful editing made the text much better.

I've been very lucky to have a special group of friends who have long pretended to be interested in my various television and book projects. Being able to share my misadventures with them on Friday evenings is an important part of what makes this fun. Terry, John III, Lee, and John Jr.—collectively the POETS Club—have long shared the philosophy expressed in song by that contemporary poet Jimmy Buffet: "If we couldn't laugh, we would all go insane."

Mostly, I want to thank my wife, Joan, who never seems to have any doubts that this will all work out, and my son, Andy, who keeps me laughing every day. Both give me constant encouragement and motivation.

John Grant
Driftwood Productions

Introduction

MANY PEOPLE HAVE A SPECIAL CONNECTION WITH TRAINS, a romantic, almost magical attraction. Often it dates back to some childhood experience or distant memory. Sometimes it is only a vague sensation, but almost always it is a happy feeling. This explains part of the appeal of train travel, but there is so much more.

With train travel, the going is as important as the getting there. The train glides along at a rhythm that allows you to become immersed in the landscape. It provides an opportunity to experience the out of the ordinary, the unexpected. While you won't find something new around every bend in the tracks, there are plenty of surprises and new experiences to be enjoyed when you ride the rails—like stopping for a grizzly bear to cross the tracks in the Alaskan wilderness, or cruising along the Pacific Ocean on rails that seem to surf the waves, or spending the day glued to the window as the train curves through strange and remote canyons of the Rocky Mountains.

Traveling through the towns and the countryside by train, you get a "behind-the-scenes" look at America. As folklorist Nick Spitzer told us when we filmed the "American South by Rail" television program for PBS, "You're moving at a wonderfully mellow pace across the landscape. You see the backs of yards, you see . . . fishing camps, you see little dance halls and honky-tonks in the crossroads of towns."

The wide windows of the train offer a remarkable and rare perspective from which to examine areas that are less traveled and occasionally places that can only be seen from the train. In addition to the dramatic vistas, train travelers also can witness wildlife at close proximity. "Today, we saw a golden eagle sitting on a fence post right next to the train," rail lecturer John Borneman reported during the "Rockies by Rail" trip. "Most of these people had never seen a golden eagle before. And we saw a mule deer right along the side of the train. You never know what you're going to see, and it's really exciting."

Most railroads in North America were built for commerce, not for tourism. Leisure travel wasn't even a consideration when railroads like the *Chihuahua al Pacifico Railway* and the *Alaska Railroad* were constructed. Today tourism is what keeps many trains running. "Train travel is so much fun because you're not having to worry about driving and being somewhere," says Matthew Wheeler, whose photographs of Via Rail's *Skeena* train are featured in "The Canadian Rockies" chapter. "This dome is like a traveling village," he says, referring to the train's bright glass-domed cars. "It's just an instantly constructed little place where you meet people from all over the world and they have fascinating stories they tell you."

Throughout *Great American Rail Journeys* you'll meet lots of people like Matthew Wheeler, John Borneman, and Nick Spitzer. They are among dozens of what we call "local storytellers," people who share their enthusiasm and love for trains and for the places we visit along the tracks. On

MATTHEW G. WHEELER

Film crew in the Canadian Rockies

these journeys you'll also meet the delightful tour guides of the *Alaska Railroad*, the remarkable chefs of the *American Orient Express*, the friendly Mexican staff of the *Sierra Madre Express*, and the informative and courteous conductors onboard Amtrak and Via Rail trains.

We first encountered all of these folks during the production of programs that originally aired on public television. The TV programs form the basis for each of the eight different rail journeys featured in these pages. The trips vary in length from the forty historic miles of the *White Pass and Yukon Route Railroad* to the six-day, 1,400-mile journey on *the American Orient Express* through the American South. Some are carefully orchestrated packages designed for the traveler's ease and comfort. Others, such as the *Alaska*

Railroad or Canada's *Skeena*, can be custom tailored to suit your personal yen for adventure. At the heart of every chapter is a train journey through a beautiful and fascinating part of North America.

To enhance your reading experience, we've filled these pages with photography that captures the spectacular beauty and picturesque charm of the locations we visited. Many of the smaller photos in the book are actually taken directly from the videotapes of the television programs. Hopefully, the collection of images will give you a sense of the majesty of these unique destinations.

South Carolina's Middleton Place is featured in "The American South by Rail."

The train is a great way to see America, whether relaxing with a cup of coffee or with an evening cocktail. The history and geography of the continent pass by your giant, moving picture window, providing a glimpse into the isolated culture of Mexico's Tarahumara Indians, an exploration of the madness that drove tens of thousand of gold rushers to the Klondike, an appreciation of the history and legends that date back centuries along the Hudson River, and much more. Each of these trips offers the patient and inquisitive traveler an opportunity to have a singular travel experience, to discover something new about America—and about himself or herself.

We hope you have a good time learning about a few of the best train journeys in North America. Have a nice trip.

Trip Profile

THE TRAIN:
The comfortable coaches of the state-owned Alaska Railroad, which features some of the best on-train guides and services of any train in North America. Coaches contain large, comfortable reclining seats and have oversized windows.

THE ROUTE:
The Denali Star *is a 356-mile trip between Anchorage and Fairbanks, Alaska's two largest cities.*

DURATION OF THE TRIP:
The Denali Star *makes the trip between Anchorage and Fairbanks in about twelve hours, all of it in daylight during the summer. Passengers can create their own multi-day itineraries that include overnight stops at places like Talkeetna and Denali National Park.*

HIGHLIGHTS:
• *The trip traverses spectacular wilderness scenery with frequent views from the train of Mount McKinley, the highest mountain in North America.*

• *The train stops at Talkeetna, a genuine frontier town that offers such activities as flight-seeing trips to Mount McKinley.*

• *The major stop on the route is Denali National Park, where you can see grizzly bears and other wild species roaming in their natural environment.*

It is said that it would take more than a lifetime to see all of Alaska and visitors to the Last Frontier must first contend with its vastness. But for those who are willing to settle for just a portion of this magnificent state and want to see it in an intimate, comfortable way, the Alaska railroad is a good place to start. A ribbon of timbers and steel,

THE ALASKA RAIL

MEANDERS THROUGH MOUNTAINS AND VALLEYS,

passing frontier towns, giant glaciers, and tangled rivers. From Anchorage to Fairbanks, the train weaves a glorious thread through a rich tapestry of uninterrupted wilderness scenery. "I like to show the state off," says Alaska Railroad senior conductor Harry Ross. "There's nothing more beautiful than the scenery up here in Alaska." Looming over the entire journey is Denali, or the "high one," as Native Americans call Mount McKinley. North America's highest mountain is an awe-inspiring backdrop for this trip on the Alaska Railroad's appropriately named *Denali Star* line.

ROAD

Early efforts to build a railroad in Alaska were plagued by financial problems and delays. Finally, in 1912, Congress initiated a plan to build a railroad link between the port of Seward and the Alaska interior. Fairbanks was chosen as the northern terminus.

The rail line was built against seemingly insurmountable odds, with track laid in many areas that seemed impassable. Construction of the railroad started at both Seward and Fairbanks. Construction camps grew into section stations where crews and their families lived and worked on the railroad. Ship Creek was chosen as the headquarters for the Alaskan Engineering Commission, and within a year a remarkable tent city of more than 2,000 railroad workers was created. In 1915 Ship Creek became Anchorage. On July 15, 1923, President and Mrs. Warren G. Harding traveled to Nenana to drive the Golden Spike commemorating the completion of the Alaska Railroad. Within a few weeks passenger and freight service was running between Seward and Fairbanks.

Since 1985 the state of Alaska has owned and operated the railroad, which covers more than 500 miles from tidewater at Whittier and Seward to Anchorage and through the heart of Alaska to Fairbanks. No other railroad in North America is quite like the Alaska Railroad. Billing itself as "America's only full-service railroad," it offers both freight and passenger service year-round. The railroad hauls a diverse freight load of natural resources such as coal, gravel, logs, and petroleum products. It is also one of the state's top tourist attractions, with more than 600,000 people riding its rails every year, most of them during the summer tourist season.

One of the special aspects of traveling on the Alaska Railroad is getting to know the people who work on the train. "I've traveled quite a bit," says brakeman Warren Redfearn. "I've been in forty-seven of the fifty states and in several countries. But the pull always is to be back here with the bears and the moose and the sheep. I just love the lifestyle, the remoteness." This veteran railroad employee is eager to share his passion with others. "My favorite part of working on the railroad is sharing the Alaska that I love with the people that ride the train, trying to show them the moose, the bear, Mount McKinley," Warren continues. "You'd think I'd tire of it after as many trips as I've done. But every time I see the mountain I get thrilled because the passengers are getting a thrill. It's an awesome sight."

Brakeman Warren Redfearn

The Alaska Railroad's *Denali Star* runs for 356 miles between Anchorage and Fairbanks, the state's two largest cities. Traveling at a leisurely pace, the train takes about twelve hours to make the trip. During peak summer months, the train runs daily in both directions. The *Denali Star* provides an opportunity to see a big chunk of wilderness, visit a fascinating Alaskan frontier town, and survey the wildlife at the state's most popular national park. In fact, spotting wildlife is an important activity on this trip, both from the train and later at Denali National Park. Passengers commonly see some of Alaska's abundant wildlife not far from trackside, and the train often slows to give everyone a chance to see both the animals and special features of their habitat. Moose, caribou, fox, bald eagles, the occasional grizzly bear, and impressive beaver dams are prime attractions in these parts.

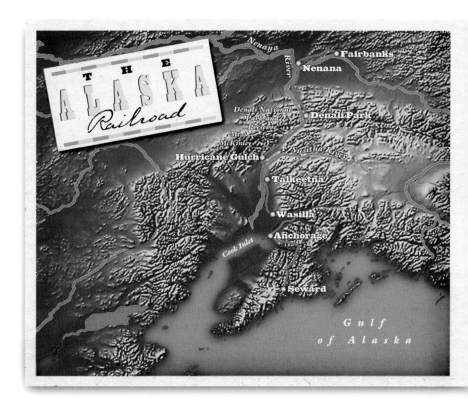

Your *Denali Star* rail adventure begins in Anchorage, Alaska's largest city. About a quarter of a million people—nearly half of Alaska's population—reside here. Actually located at milepost 114.3 on the Alaska Railroad, because the line starts in Seward to the south, Anchorage began as a railroad construction base and saw boom times as a military staging area during both world wars. Despite that history, Alaska's great natural beauty is evident in Anchorage, with mountains visible on every horizon on a clear day. Anchorage is an easy place to get around, and tourist shops and other interesting attractions can provide reasons to linger a short while. But Anchorage, like Fairbanks at the northern terminus of the railroad, is not what this trip is about. The lure is what lies in between.

Bald eagles and other wildlife are commonly seen along the route.

At the height of the summer tourist season, travelers from all over the world arrive at the Anchorage Station. For many this is the trip of a lifetime—a romantic adventure to the edge of civilization. Like Jack London, Robert Service, and so many others before them, the tourists answer the call of one of the last great wildernesses on earth. "Welcome to the Alaska Railway," says guide Tania Matlock. "In just a few minutes, we will begin boarding our north-

Alaska Railroad Engine #1 is prominently displayed in front of the station in Anchorage to honor former and current employees of the Alaska Railroad.

bound train to Wasilla, Talkeetna, Denali National Park, and Fairbanks." You can choose from several ways to ride the Alaska Railroad. Individual tour companies attach their own dome and diner cars to the rear of the regularly scheduled Alaska Railroad train, and many of the tour company passengers arrive in Alaska via cruise ships at Seward and follow a fixed schedule. The Alaska Railroad welcomes independent travelers and will even help to make reservations for lodging and other activities along the route. Just call the toll-free number (see Appendix) for assistance in planning your own itinerary along the train route. For the two railroad programs produced for public television, we traveled in the latter way—as independent passengers riding the distinctive dark blue and bright yellow cars of the Alaska Railroad.

On the first day of the journey, the Alaska Railroad pulls out of Anchorage at 8:15 A.M. The passenger coaches are well maintained, clean, and comfortable. Each coach features reclining seats with lots of legroom and large picture windows. Meals are available throughout the trip in two dining cars, and the menu features Alaskan entrees, well prepared and served by a friendly staff. Only a short distance out of Anchorage, the train leaves most traces of civilization behind and enters the pristine wilderness of the Alaska Range, the magnificent 600-mile arc of mountains that divides south-central Alaska from the interior plateau.

Once underway you'll experience one of the delights that makes the Alaska Railroad such a unique train experience. "When people come to Alaska and they're on the Alaska Railroad, they receive a lot of personal attention," says guide Tania Matlock. She is one of a handful of young Alaskans selected to be railway tour guides, the pride of the Alaska Railroad's passenger service for nearly two decades. The tour guides are high school students chosen through a highly competitive process. "They go through a class that lasts about four months and learn all the different aspects about Alaska," says conductor Harry Ross. "We put these tour guides on our trains, they learn the different scenery along the way, and then they relay information to the passengers and answer questions. It's just a wonderful program." You'll learn more from the tour guides about the railroad, Alaskan history, and wildlife than from any guidebook.

In addition to its marvelous staff, the Alaska Railroad provides an excellent route map that helps you know where you are and what to look for along the way. Milepost signs on trees and telephone poles are easy to read from the train. You can also buy a more detailed milepost guide in the gift shop at the station or on board the train.

Just five miles north of Anchorage, the train passes through Elmendorf Air Force Base, Alaska's largest air base. Fighter jets are frequently parked alongside the runway, and jets can occasionally be seen taking off or landing. Elmendorf was built during World War II, during a time that saw a significant increase in military activity in Alaska. The Alaska Railroad became a critical component for transporting construction materials and troops. Civilian guards were placed at all of the principal railroad bridges, trestles, and terminal yards.

Harry Ross

The Alaska Railroad features a select group of rigorously trained Alaskan high school students who serve as onboard tour guides.

John Grant

The train crosses the Eagle River, milky from glacial silt.

Military guards rode on freight trains carrying military supplies. The heavy use of the railroad during the war left the track in poor condition, so in the late 1940s the government began a rehabilitation program that upgraded major portions of the route.

A few miles farther up the track, the Eagle River drains from Eagle Glacier in the Chugach Mountains. The water is very milky due to the glacial silt it carries, but it is a popular stream for local canoers and kayakers in the summer. It is rare that some wildlife isn't spotted during the train journey, and this early stretch is an especially good place to watch for moose.

Less than half an hour north of Anchorage, your first glimpse of Mount McKinley materializes. Weather permitting, you'll see the giant mountain through the trees. If clouds obscure the view, don't despair. This is just the first of many opportunities you'll have to see Mount McKinley from the train. Near Birchwood, the Knik Arm begins to parallel the path of the train. The Knik Arm, a cove-like, narrow body of water, is located at the northern end of Cook Inlet, which has the second highest tides in the world, sometimes reaching thirty-five to forty feet. Only the Bay of Fundy in Nova Scotia has greater tidal variations. If the tide is out, you'll see gleaming mudflats that stretch for

Framed by the Chugach Mountain Range, the Denali Star *heads north from Anchorage.*

hundreds of feet. Visitors are warned not to walk on the mud because the tide flows back in so quickly that you can get caught in the mud and drown.

Shortly after leaving the Knik Arm, the train crosses a bridge over the Eklutna River and enters an area of towering mountain ranges. Nearby, the Eklutna Indian Village is the site of a cemetery with colorful "spirit houses" built on top of graves to preserve the souls buried there. One of the oldest surviving examples of Russian architecture in the area is St. Nicholas Church, a log structure built around the mid-1800s. Inside are icons brought from Russia. The train doesn't stop at Eklutna, but if you'd like to visit, it's only a half-hour drive up the Glenn Highway from Anchorage.

Pulling away from the Eklutna River, the tracks pass under the Glenn Highway as the *Denali Star* begins its passage across the scenic and agriculturally rich Matanuska Valley, home of world-record-winning vegetables and the center of agriculture for south-central Alaska. The growing season here is only about three months, but record crops result from the long hours of daylight during the summer, reaching nineteen hours at the seasonal peak. The Alaska State Fair is held in nearby Palmer, where it is not unusual to find fifty-pound cabbages on display. Matanuska, now just a milepost, was once a thriving town and supply center on the rail line. A branch line ran north thirty-eight miles through the Matanuska coalfields, which provided fuel for the Alaska Railroad's steam engines. Around 1917 enough coal could be taken from the Matanuska area to supply the railroad's needs on the entire route. Prior to that time coal was shipped north from Seattle for use on the railroad.

Around 9:45 A.M., the train makes its first scheduled stop at Wasilla. Founded in 1917 as a stop on the Alaska Railroad, Wasilla became an important supply center for the gold-mining settlements farther north up the Susitna River. Now Wasilla is the headquarters of the famed Iditarod Sled Dog Race that runs every March from here to Nome. The headquarters is open year-round, with displays of dogsleds, clothing, trail gear, and video highlights of previous races. If you want to explore this quaint, cozy Alaska town and the surrounding areas, the best method is probably to take the short and scenic ninety-minute drive from Anchorage as a day trip or even spend an overnight before getting on the Alaska Railroad.

Leaving Wasilla, the train passes through an isolated area of abandoned homesteads and small towns. Willow is one of these, better known because it almost became the state capital in the 1970s. In those years a movement was afoot to change the capital from Juneau to a more accessible location near the major population centers of Anchorage and Fairbanks. Although they voted to move the capital to Willow, citizens failed to approve the billions of dollars needed to make the move and the effort failed. Alaska's capital remains in Juneau, the only water-locked state capital in the United States—that is, the only one with no road access by land. The city is served by daily air and marine ferry service.

The Susitna River parallels the rails for the next seventy miles, both following the same path north along the Talkeetna Mountains. The Susitna, a native word meaning "sandy river," begins in the Susitna and MacLaren Glaciers more than 100 miles east in the Alaska Range and is navigable for seventy-five miles upstream from Knik Arm to Talkeetna. Salmon migrate upstream hundreds of miles via this important river, entering the smaller tributaries and struggling even farther before spawning.

About three hours after leaving Anchorage, you encounter one of the best scenic views of the trip at milepost 224. If the weather is clear enough to see Mount McKinley, the train usually slows where the view is uninterrupted by trees. Mount McKinley towers above the distant land-scape at 20,320 feet. You can see several other majestic peaks that seem dwarfed by the "high one." Mount Foraker, at 17,400 feet, is visible to the west. Mount Hunter, at 14,570 feet, sits right in front of McKinley and in bad weather is often confused for the great mountain. To the north, Mount Silverthrone sits at 13,200 feet. Eleven glaciers originate in this por-tion of the Alaska Range.

JOHN GRANT

From Anchorage to Talkeetna, the train passes tree-lined gullies and riverbeds, excellent places to look for wildlife such as moose, caribou, and even the occasional bear.

With any luck, you'll still be breathlessly awestruck by the views only a few miles farther up the track, when the *Denali Star* pulls into Talkeetna, a classic Alaskan frontier village and the base station for those attempting to climb Mount McKinley. The town was established as a trapping and gold-mining outpost, and now, as a major tourist attraction, it retains

much of its rustic frontier charm. The "downtown" is only about three square blocks, and half of the buildings are on the National Register of Historic Places. Two small museums—the Talkeetna Historical Society Museum in the old red schoolhouse and the Museum of Northern Adventure—provide tales of gold seekers, Alaskan natives, the railroad, bush pilots, and mountaineers. A free "Historical Walking Tour" brochure is available at the museums or at the downtown log cabin Visitor Center next to the hand-painted WELCOME TO BEAUTIFUL DOWNTOWN TALKEETNA sign.

The train arrives in Talkeetna at 11:15 A.M., allowing you the rest of the day and evening to see the area's attractions before reboarding the northbound train the next morning to continue your rail journey. If your schedule permits, you can plan for a few days here. Plenty of comfortable lodging options are available in Talkeetna, although some may offer fewer amenities than you may be used to in the lower forty-eight states. In recent years, a number of large, tourist-oriented lodges have opened near Talkeetna, but if you want the true Alaskan frontier experience, you should stay in "Beautiful Downtown Talkeetna." Among several good places to eat is the Talkeetna Roadhouse, a hangout for locals and mountain climbers who swear by its large portions of home-style cooking.

Talkeetna means "river of plenty" in the native language, so it's not surprising to learn that fishing charters for salmon and trout, riverboat tours, and float trips are available on the Talkeetna, Chulitna, and Susitna Rivers, which all converge nearby. River safaris offer wildlife viewing that includes bald eagles, beavers, moose, and even black bears and grizzly

bears. "What I love best about Alaska is there's not that many people and so they're really taking care to make sure that fifty years from now we'll have the same amount of wildlife and the same amount of habitat," says Margaret Salmon, who operates a guide

Margaret Salmon

and eco-tourism service on the rivers that surround Talkeetna. Margaret typifies the independent, frontier spirit that still is part of the Alaskan experience. "I love this state," she says. "It's a land of opportunity. I certainly haven't felt anyone stomping on me to hold me back, so the sky's the limit. If you've got the energy, you can pretty much go for it."

River enthusiasts are not the only outdoor explorers who fill the rooms in Talkeetna hostelries. Mountain climbers from around the world come to Talkeetna to register at the National Park Service Ranger Station before challenging Mount McKinley. Inspirational in its beauty and awesome in its

scale, the mountain is a terrifying adversary for those who dare to challenge its formidable heights. More than 22,000 people have attempted to climb McKinley, but only about half have been successful. More than ninety climbers have died in the effort. The oldest person to make the summit was seventy-one; the youngest was a twelve-year-old Korean boy. Commonly cited as the highest peak in North

A float trip down one of the rivers near Talkeetna.

America, the mountain is considered by many to be the highest in the world when measured from the 2,000-foot lowlands near Wonder Lake to its summit. Mount McKinley creates its own weather and is known to climbers as the coldest mountain in North America. The summit temperature never rises above freezing, and hurricane-force winds can arise suddenly and literally blow an unwary climber off the mountain's precipitous ridges.

Despite the generally relaxed, pleasant atmosphere of Talkeetna, the sense of danger on the mountain is very real. While our television crew was having dinner one evening at the Talkeetna Roadhouse, a park ranger came in with a dazed and frozen-looking climber who had been stuck on the mountain for several days without food. The climber's friend didn't make it, having disappeared off the mountain in a sudden violent storm. We had seen climbers just like this man only a few days earlier enjoying the clear cold weather at the Denali base camp. On the day that this man was facing a life-or-death situation on the mountain, the weather in Talkeenta was perfectly clear and pleasant, with no indication of the life-threatening conditions causing havoc at higher elevations.

Of course, you don't have to be a mountain climber to experience Mount McKinley up close. "It's going to be a gorgeous day up here," says Buck Woods, a pilot for one of the flight services that operate Mount McKinley sight-seeing tours from the airport at Talkeetna. He will fly you

©DAVID MUENCH

up to the mountain and bring you back with memories that will last a lifetime. "We'll wander up here and see if we can get through this pass. Looks
like we can," Buck says with a matter-of-fact attitude that reassures his
passengers. "You're looking at the largest vertical rise on earth. We're looking right at the south summit: 20,320 feet." Buck has been flying in
Alaska for more than fifteen years but he never tires of this trip. "The view
changes every day. The mountain changes every day. I don't think there is
any such thing as a routine flight, but it's sure a lot of fun."

If you're looking for even more adventure, Buck will land the plane
right on Mount McKinley for a closer inspection. "Okay," Buck says, "we'll
take an orbit around base camp and we'll land." The Denali base camp is
located on the Kahiltna Glacier at an altitude of 7,500 feet. Most climbers
begin and end their ascents of Mount McKinley from this spot. Annie
Duquette, better known as "Glacier Annie," runs the base camp for the air
charter operators. "I get to meet people from all over the world. It's really

Mount McKinley at sunrise

Buck Woods

interesting for me," Annie says. "Living on a glacier is a lot different from living on pavement or soil." Even long-time mountain dweller Annie can't squelch her enthusiasm for this experience. She makes it clear that a flight-seeing trip to the Mount McKinley base camp is exhilarating for all travelers.

Annie Duquette

With lifetime memories of Talkeetna and Mount McKinley frozen in place, we board the Alaska Railroad heading to Denali National Park. We cross the Talkeetna River and start a gradual climb toward the Continental Divide. Though the ever-looming Mount McKinley comes into view several times as the train journeys away from Talkeetna, you may also notice that the landscape begins to change in this area, with more vegetation and forests. If you take the trip in July, for instance, it is impossible to miss the fireweed, the brilliant pink flowers that line the route.

Around milepost 233 you may also notice large beaver lodges near the tracks. This area is on an ancient floodplain of the Susitna River. Beavers are very active along this swampy stretch, building with the abundant birch trees. Within this portion of the journey, you may also see several paths leading away from the tracks. These lead to isolated cabins in the

wilderness. The train is the only form of transportation into this area and serves as the only lifeline to civilization for the people who live here. Residents living along the tracks or in the nearby roadless foothills can flag down the train anywhere along the route. This service is provided by very

few other trains in the country. Visitors to Alaska can also ride the local flag train to gain an intimate perspective on the Alaska bush country.

It is in these parts that you truly gain an appreciation for the Last Frontier, as the train continues on its path through isolated wilderness. The Indian River Canyon seems as far away from civilization as one might get. The *Star* crosses the Indian River several times, and occasionally you can spot salmon in the river or a rare angler along the banks. As the train

THE FLAG TRAIN

The Alaska Railroad's Hurricane Turn *train* is one of the best ways to have a true Alaskan wilderness bush experience. It is one of the last flag trains in North America. "This train is specifically for the locals and tourists that might want to get out and get a unique perspective of the railroad," explains conductor Eugene Owens. The railroad is the only access for a fifty-mile stretch between Talkeetna and Hurricane. "We make stops all along the way for people that have cabins or people that live in this area, stopping and unloading food and baggage, and that's what's so unique about this run," Owens says. The train stops when someone literally flags it down—often by using a white cloth—as it passes.

While it is mostly used by locals who live along the route, tourists also ride the train. "We got a hot tip from a fly fisherman that the Indian River is the place to go for rainbow, so we're headed up there," says a tourist looking for a less crowded fishing spot. "We're not exactly sure where we're going, but we know the conductor's going to tell us." At milepost 269 the train stops, and the conductor helps the couple unload their fishing gear. "There is some beautiful-looking water," he says. "Absolutely gorgeous. Right in there's a good bend, and if you go down this way on the other side of the bridge, there's a good spot. You know what you're doing, you'll find them."

A few hours later the flag train makes its way back south, and the train staff is on the lookout for the pair of adventurous fishermen. Sure enough, they are standing along the tracks at milepost 269, looking very satisfied with their wilderness experience. "She had a fifteen-inch rainbow caught, photographed, and released before I even had a fly on," chuckles the fisherman as he climbs back on board the flag train.

The Hurricane Turn operates four days a week, Thursday through Sunday, during the summer. The train is a single car with few amenities, so you'll need to bring everything you need with you. The flag train leaves from Talkeetna at 12:15 P.M. At Hurricane, the train turns around for the return trip to Talkeetna. The round-trip of fifty-five miles takes about five and a half hours, and you can get dropped off and picked up anywhere along the tracks. If you want to take the Hurricane Turn, you can catch the regular Denali Star to Talkeetna and then jump on the flag train for a true Alaskan rail adventure.

Hurricane Turn, one of the few flag trains in the United States, serves the most remote stretch along the rail corridor.

The conductor checks to see where passengers want to be dropped off.

Guide Tania Matlock points out scenic highlights along the route.

approaches Hurricane, a stretch of several miles offers more good views of Mount McKinley. At milepost 279, McKinley is only forty-six miles away, the closest the railroad gets to the mountain. "Ladies and gentlemen, in just a few moments we're going to be coming up to Hurricane Gulch," says train guide Tania Matlock. "This bridge was built in 1921 by the American Bridge Company. They started on either side and worked towards the middle, using an aerial tram for construction." The train slows to cross the 918-foot Hurricane Gulch trestle, the most expensive and most difficult-to-build trestle on the entire route. At 296 feet above the creek below, and with tremendous scenery on all sides, it provides one of the route's best photo opportunities.

Don't put the camera or the binoculars away too fast once you cross the trestle, though. Soon the *Denali Star* races on toward Broad Pass, at 2,300 feet the lowest pass across the Alaska Range. For the next several miles, you travel through a beautiful valley surrounded by jagged peaks. The valley floor and the summer weather provide the perfect environment for blueberries, which attract wildlife to the area. You may be able to catch sight of black bears or other species as you pass by. Before long, the train reaches Summit. With an elevation of 2,363 feet, this is the highest point on the Alaska Railroad, yet it is the lowest rail crossing of the Continental Divide in the Rocky Mountains. If you watch closely as the train passes Carlo around milepost 333, you'll see a log cabin and the food cache of a local resident. The cache is a log structure built on stilts to keep bear and other pests away from the food.

More than two hundred miles north of Anchorage, the *Denali Star* crosses the Riley Creek Bridge, second highest on the railroad, and arrives at Denali Station. The arrival of the train in late afternoon sets off a frenzy of activity. Only a few minutes earlier, the station was empty, virtually abandoned. Now dozens of buses and vans belonging to local tour companies and hotels are lined up at the station. Hundreds of people stand behind rope barriers waiting to board the train while hundreds of others are getting off and looking for some sign of recognition. Hotel and tour representatives hold up small signs and point people in the right direction. In an amazingly short amount of time, everyone is gone and the station is quiet again until the arrival of the next train full of tourists.

The crowds are arriving to see the national park, an area set aside in 1917 to be preserved in its natural state. The original purpose of the preserve was to protect large mammals, not the majestic mountain for which the park was originally named. In 1980 the park was expanded to cover an area larger than the state of Massachusetts, and it was renamed Denali National Park and Preserve. At one time, the railroad or bush planes were the only ways to get to the park, but the opening of the George Parks

Nearly everyone who takes the park road in Denali National Park sees wildlife. But seeing Mt. McKinley takes luck, as it is obscured by clouds about sixty-five percent of the time.

JOHN GRANT

Highway in 1972 allowed access to the area by automobile. Now Denali is the most accessible and heavily visited national park in Alaska. You should expect crowds if you visit during the peak tourist season.

If you choose to stay here awhile, you'll find a wide variety of accommodations at Denali National Park—everything from hotels and motels to rustic streamside cabins. Most are clustered near or within a few miles of the entrance to the park. If you call the Alaska Railroad reservations number, their staff will help you sort out some of the lodging options and even make reservations for you. A travel agent can also be helpful. Just be sure to check that the amenities of importance to you are available at the lodging you book. Without a car you may feel a little isolated, but there is an effective, if sometimes overworked, shuttle bus system to get you around to the major locations. This is just a great place to slow down and enjoy the amazing sights and sounds of a true wilderness experience.

Access to Denali National Park is strictly limited to hikers and tour buses. No cars are allowed beyond mile 14 on the park road. Most visitors to Denali take a bus tour that provides an excellent opportunity to see the park's geography and wildlife. The trip into Denali's interior is an unforgettable experience of tundra, braided glacial streams, mountain vistas, wildlife, and, on a clear day, views of Mount McKinley. Animals roam freely throughout the park, and you can see caribou, moose, fox, grizzly bear, mountain goats, and over a hundred varieties of birds. While there are no guarantees, nearly all visitors see some wildlife and most see a grizzly, albeit at a good, safe distance. The great feature of Denali National Park is that the animals are in charge and you get to see them in their natural environment doing what they do on any ordinary day in the wilderness. Even the tour buses wait for animals to cross the road.

Shuttle bus tours range from five and a half hours to thirteen hours. A popular eight-hour trip goes to the Eielson Visitor Center at mile 66. This stop has an observation deck, picnic tables, an indoor visitor's center, and a bookstore. The center is perched on the tundra slopes and provides good opportunities for observing wildlife. If you are more adventurous, leave on a day hike from this central point. You can spend as much time in the park as you like—just be sure to check when the last bus leaves for the day. The shuttle bus system allows you to get on and off buses anywhere along the route. Bus drivers or a guide point out highlights and lead in the lookout for wildlife. It is always exciting when someone spots an animal and everyone else strains to see it. Be sure to pack a lunch, snacks, and beverages as no facilities within the park offer these staples. You may also want to bring binoculars along, since most of the wildlife you'll see is at a distance.

Jerryne Cole

Wally Cole

Of the more than six million acres that make up Denali, the vast majority of it is backcountry without trails, bridges, or other developments. A few lodging accommodations lie deep within the park at Kantishna at the end of the ninety-mile road. They offer an unforgettable wilderness experience. "I think the reason we exist here in Denali National Park is to give the more adventurous of the folks who travel here an alternative to what is the norm in terms of accommodations and experience," explains Jerryne Cole, who owns and operates Camp Denali with her husband, Wally. "People come here to see the mountains," Wally says, "and this is one of the unique places on the globe where you can look out your cabin and view the mountain right between your toes, if you position yourself accordingly in your bed."

Founded in 1951, Camp Denali is the oldest tourist operation in Denali National Park. Jerryne and Wally bought the place in 1975 with a commitment to preserve its rustic heritage. The accommodations are spartan but comfortable, and the food is excellent. Cabins don't have running water, electricity, or indoor plumbing. The main lodge at Camp Denali is a homey gathering place, warmed by a cast-iron stove. A library is crammed with books on Alaska's nature and wildlife, and a resource center is full of skulls, pelts, casts of animal tracks, and a plant collection. For the slightly less adventurous, nearby North Face Lodge, also owned by the Coles, is a more modern facility equipped with every amenity. Both require a minimum stay of several days, and both offer great views of the mountain and the wilderness.

"The founders of Camp Denali wanted to establish a place where people could come and get a feel for the land," Wally says, "just to experience Alaska." Guests are free to explore on their own, choosing from such activities as hiking, mountain biking, and canoeing on the lake. The lodge also provides a knowledgeable staff of naturalist guides who take groups out

into the bush each day. "We want people to become comfortable who have never experienced anything like this before," Jerryne adds, "and go home with new eyes about how comfortable they can be in a wilderness setting."

As if this fact hasn't become obvious to you, Mount McKinley has been called the Alaskan landscape's most impressive feature. After seeing the framed peak, visitors are quickly overcome by the same sense of awe that inspired the early Athabascan natives to hold the mountain sacred. After even a short visit to Denali National Park, you come away with memories to last a lifetime.

The final leg of this rail journey takes you from Denali to Fairbanks, the north end of the main line and the northernmost railroad terminus in North America. When it leaves the boundary of Denali National Park, the train enters the beautiful Nenana River Canyon, passing through tunnels and along rocky ledges that offer great views of the raging river below. The canyon was a major problem for builders of the Alaska Railroad. The large amounts of gravel in the area made the soil unstable, and landslides were a constant fear. Blasting tunnels through the canyon was also necessary to clear the way for the tracks. As the *Denali Star* leaves the canyon, the terrain opens and the weather and vegetation change. Aspen trees become more prevalent as the terrain flattens. Soon you are in the rain shadow of the Alaska Range, where it is more arid than in the land south of the mountains. Dark coal seams are visible in the exposed rock near Healy, the center of the Nenana River Coal Field. The railroad carries tons of coal from Healy to the port at Seward for shipment to Korea.

One more thrill awaits you as the *Denali Star* draws closer to its final destination: the 702-foot-long Mears Memorial Bridge, which spans the Tanana River. The steel structure is one of the world's longest single-span bridges and the last major bridge to be built on the Alaska Railroad route. At the bridge's west end, on July 15, 1923, President Warren G. Harding drove the Golden Spike that marked the completion of the railroad. Watch below for Athabascan fish wheels along the banks of the river. The current

COAST AND COUNTRY
DAY TRIPS BY RAIL

In addition to the route between Anchorage and Fairbanks, the Alaska Railroad offers two other regularly scheduled trips. While neither compares with the overall experience of the Denali Star, both are terrific rail adventures. You can make either of these round-trips in a single day with plenty of time for sight-seeing, including wonderful cruises that depart from Seward and Whittier.

Some consider the Coastal Classic route from Anchorage to Seward one of the most scenic train trips in the world. Dramatically different from the northern route to Fairbanks, yet no less captivating, the landscape along this run includes spectacular mountains reminiscent of the Swiss Alps. You will be entranced as the train passes within a half mile of three majestic glaciers and travels over gorges and past several waterfalls. Many of these sights and others cannot be seen except from the train. "We see something different every day, and it's just beautiful," says senior conductor Harry Ross. The Coastal Classic leaves Anchorage at 6:45 A.M., arriving in Seward around 11:00 A.M. The northbound return train doesn't depart until 6:00 P.M., so you have plenty of time to explore this beautiful port city.

Located in the Kenai Mountains at the northern end of Resurrection Bay, Seward is an ice-free port with a relatively mild climate. The Kenai Peninsula is one of the most beautiful places on earth, and one of the best ways to see it is on a half-day cruise that leaves from Seward. One of the best trips is the Resurrection Bay Park Ranger Cruise, which offers passengers the chance to see puffins, eagles, sea lions, otters, and whales.

The Glacier Discovery is the newest of the Alaska Railroad's routes, running between Anchorage and the port community of Whittier. The train leaves Anchorage at 9:00 A.M. and arrives in Whittier at 11:30 A.M., allowing plenty of time for exploration before the return train departs for Anchorage at 5:45 P.M. Whittier itself offers few activities, but it is a good starting point for discovering the treasures of Prince William Sound. Several half-day cruises provide views of towering glaciers, spectacular waterfalls, and close-up marine wildlife.

CALVIN W. HALL

The trip from Anchorage to Seward offers terrific views of glaciers that can only be seen from the train.

propels the paddles and catches salmon swimming upstream to spawn.

The scenery from here to Fairbanks remains beautiful, if slightly less spectacular. This is a time when you can reflect on your magical journey through the heart of Alaska. First-time visitors to the state may begin to gain a sense of the size and majesty of this land. Amazingly, even though you've traveled through more than 300 miles of wilderness, you've seen only a tiny part of Alaska. Look on any map of Alaska and you'll be surprised at how small the distance seems from Anchorage to Fairbanks. Much more of Alaska remains to be explored and enjoyed. With the fading, rhythmic sounds of the rails and with warm memories of the spell "The Great Land" has cast, this Alaskan rail adventure comes to an end. In 1899 Harry Gannett, the chief geographer for the U.S. Geological Survey, was part of an expedition of scientists, writers, photographers, and artists to visit Alaska. At the end of the trip, Gannett wrote in his journal: "If you are old, go by all means; but if you are young, wait. The scenery of Alaska is much grander than anything else of the kind in the world, and it is not well to dull one's capacity for enjoyment by seeing the finest first."

Trip Profile

THE TRAIN:

Amtrak's Adirondack provides comfortable seating and large windows for excellent views of the scenery. Three café cars provide lunch, drinks, and snacks. No overnight accommodations are available on this train.

THE ROUTE:

The Adirondack travels nearly 400 miles between New York City and Montreal along the eastern border of New York state and into Canada's Quebec province.

DURATION OF THE TRIP:

The Adirondack takes about ten hours to travel from New York City to Montreal, with eighteen regularly scheduled stops between these two cities. There are daily departures in both directions.

HIGHLIGHTS:

Three dramatic sections contribute to the unforgettable nature of this trip. The first is the romantic Hudson River Valley, with one of the largest collections of historic landmarks and architectural attractions in the country. The second is the Adirondack Mountains, the largest park in the lower 48 states. The third is the incredibly beautiful and peaceful Lake Champlain.

Despite the fact that its pathway links two of North America's most exciting cities, the Adirondack may be one of Amtrak's best-kept secrets. Few travelers seem to realize that in a single day this train covers nearly 400 miles of what one nineteenth-century American writer called "nature's greatest panorama."

THE ADIRO

EVERY DAY OF THE YEAR, THE ADIRONDACK curls along the Hudson River and through the wilderness beauty of its namesake mountains before finishing its scenic cruise along the rocky banks of Lake Champlain. Competing for attention with the scenery is the enormous volume of American history, architecture, and legend tucked along the route—arguably the largest concentration of national historic landmarks and romantic landscapes in the United States. Ironically, even with ample evidence of the region's remarkable human history, stretches of this route remain much as they were before anyone arrived. The train provides a unique perspective of this region, following the route of its first explorers and earliest settlers.

NDACK

New York City to the south and Montreal at the north bracket the route of the *Adirondack,* and both offer days of exciting and sophisticated activities at the beginning and end of the trip. The straight ten-hour trip between New York City and Montreal is a relaxing, enjoyable train experience. In autumn, changing leaves create a particularly glorious backdrop, but the scenery is fabulous just about any time of the year. In fact, the winter months, when the leaves are off the trees, provide the best views of the high peaks of the Adirondack Mountains.

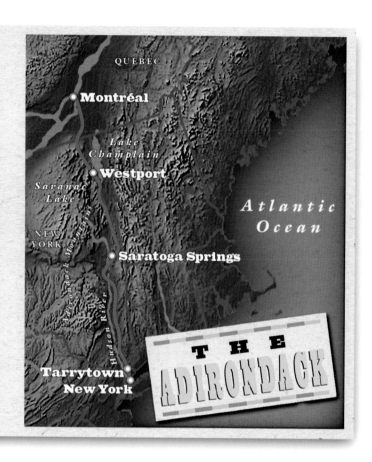

If you'd like to plan a longer excursion, the *Adirondack* makes more than a dozen stops that offer opportunities for day trips full of adventure and discovery. One of the biggest surprises of this journey may indeed be that there are actually many more fascinating places to visit than you'll likely have time for in a single trip. It's a good idea to plan your itinerary carefully ahead of time so you can coordinate the train schedule with your off-train plans and make arrangements for your transportation when you get off the train. Plenty of lodging and transportation options are available at just about every stop, so it's possible, for example, to get off the train at one stop, rent a car for a day or two, and rejoin the train at another stop farther north. The *Adirondack* helps you explore this entire area without using the often congested highways.

The *Adirondack* experience is different from some of the scenic rail journeys elsewhere in North America. The scenery along this route is more subtle than in other regions, but it is no less compelling. The beauty of the Hudson River surprises many people and is made even more enjoyable by the proximity of the rails to the water. Its picturesque splendor, its aura of history, and the lavish architecture along its banks give the Hudson River a

timeless quality spanning generations, if not eons. When the train reaches the broad expanses of Lake Champlain farther north, the tracks curve gracefully along the edge of the lake between rock ledges and open water. The sixth largest body of water in the United States, Lake Champlain is surpassed only by the five Great Lakes. In between the river and the lake is the wilderness of Adirondack State Park, the largest forest preserve in the lower forty-eight states. It too feels like a place where time has stood still. Home to the so-called Great Camps of another era, Adirondack State Park offers an almost unlimited array of recreational and touring opportunities. In all of these beautiful natural settings, from the river to the forest and onward to the lake, the *Adirondack* offers an opportunity to explore one of the most extraordinary concentrations of historic landmarks and architectural masterpieces in the United States.

Hudson Highlands, a stretch of the Hudson River Valley near Cold Springs, New York, offers some of the best scenery of the journey and is considered among the most beautiful landscapes in the country.

Amtrak conductor Rick Palmer

Your northbound journey on the *Adirondack* begins at New York City's historic Pennsylvania Station, a cavernous depot that links long-distance, commuter, and subway trains. One of the oldest and busiest rail terminals in America, it is full of energy and activity as the *Adirondack* pulls out just before ten in the morning. "Good morning, and welcome aboard the *Adirondack,*" Amtrak conductor Rick Palmer greets the day's passengers. "This is Amtrak's Empire Service from New York's Penn Station to Montreal, Quebec. You can sit back, relax, and enjoy the ride." Rick is used to the mix of passengers that ride the *Adirondack*. "We have a lot of regular riders—people who do a lot of commuting from New York up to the Adirondacks or to the Albany area. And we have first-time travelers who are just glued to the window looking out at the sights." Rick has been railroading for more than thirty years and has come to appreciate his above-average workaday surroundings. "The Hudson River Valley is very, very scenic, and it's just outside the city of New York, which makes it very interesting for people who leave the hustle and bustle of the concrete territory right into this beautiful atmosphere in less than an hour," he says. "We have a very beautiful state, especially upstate New York and the Adirondack State Park, which is absolutely gorgeous. Some of the scenes are breathtaking."

Leaving New York City, the *Adirondack* passes skyscrapers and negotiates a series of tunnels before it emerges at 125th Street, the unofficial main street of New York's famed Harlem district. The first glimpses of the Hudson River can be seen out the left side of the train, and the panorama is dominated by the gigantic George Washington Bridge, the longest suspension bridge in the world when it was completed in 1931. Today it is one of the nation's busiest bridges, carrying fourteen lanes of traffic. Across the river are the spectacular cliffs of the Palisades, some soaring higher than 800 feet above the water.

After a stop at the suburb of Yonkers, the *Adirondack* leaves New York City behind and heads into the richly historic and romantic Hudson River Valley. The Hudson River is a relatively short waterway, only 315 miles long from its headwaters at the romantically named Lake Tear in the Clouds in the Adirondack Mountains to New York Harbor. The Dutch first settled the Hudson River Valley in the early 1600s. In the eighteenth century, control of

THE TRAIN

The Adirondack continues a long tradition of rail passenger service along this route. More than a hundred years ago, the Delaware & Hudson rail line began to provide transportation for the growing number of travelers wanting a link between the city and the towns of upstate New York. The D&H operated The Laurentian until 1971 when Amtrak was established. In 1974, with financial assistance from the state of New York, Amtrak reinstituted the service as the Adirondack route. Today the Adirondack carries on the nostalgic and romantic service from the Hudson Valley through the Champlain Valley to Montreal and continues to be supported by the New York Department of Transportation as a unique travel experience. Most riders of the Adirondack are of the non-business, tourist, and recreational variety, and yet the train is of great importance to upstate New York because it is the only regularly scheduled public transportation available for many of the local communities.

Whether they travel for practical or pleasurable reasons, all passengers enjoy the comfort of the Adirondack's refurbished Heritage cars. Recent improvements include overhead storage and the addition of ski racks and more luggage space. The new cars offer a smooth ride, and larger windows provide excellent views of the scenery along the route. Three café-lounge cars have names that reflect the route—"L'Auberge Laurentian," "Saratoga Inn," and "Adirondack Lodge"—and menus are listed in both French and English to suit both American and Canadian travelers. You may even get a sense of the "flavor" of the region just by sampling the food and beverage selections that are products of the Champlain Valley, such as cheesecake baked by the nuns of the New Skete Order.

THE ADIRONDACK

DELAWARE AND HUDSON RAILWAY
COMPANY

The Adirondack operates once a day, seven days a week, in both directions between New York City and Montreal. Monday through Saturday, it runs a regular schedule with a morning departure and early evening arrival, but on Sundays the southbound train has a later departure from Montreal. As a result, for much of the year the Sunday train passes through the Hudson River Valley after dark, so be sure to plan well if you're hoping to see the scenery. Reservations are required on the Adirondack, and United States citizens crossing into Canada require some form of identification. Be sure to carry a passport, voter registration card, or birth certificate—a driver's license is not sufficient.

If you are interested in just the trip through the Hudson River Valley, Amtrak's Ethan Allen Express is worth considering. Financed in part by the Vermont Department of Transportation, this train follows the same route as the Adirondack between New York City and Fort Edwards/Glens Falls, before turning east into Vermont. The New York City to Fort Edwards trip takes less than four hours and covers the most scenic areas of the Hudson River Valley. The entire route between New York City and Rutland, Vermont, takes only five hours. Fall is an especially good time to take this route, which includes the changing colors of the Hudson River Valley as well as the foliage of Vermont's Green Mountains. If you'd like a carefree route to snowy slopes, ask in winter about the Ethan Allen Express all-inclusive ski packages.

this water highway meant control of
the country, and thus it's not surprising
that one-third of the battles during the
Revolutionary War were fought along
the Hudson River. Important also as an
avenue of commerce, the Hudson has
long been the scene of significant
events in maritime history. The world's
first commercially successful steam-
powered boat, for instance, operated on
the Hudson River in 1807. Military
and commercial interests did nothing,
however, to alter the aesthetic allure of
this magnificent waterway. Inspirational to the artists of the famed
Hudson River School, the river's beauty
has been captured on canvas by generations of painters. Also the setting for
the tales of Rip Van Winkle and the
headless horseman, much of the
Hudson River Valley retains the ambience of centuries past.

The early part of the *Adirondack*'s journey is a particularly beautiful section where the tracks pass through the Hudson Highlands for about fifteen
miles, an area of the river that looks much as it did when Henry Hudson
explored it nearly four centuries ago. From a window seat on the train, you
might see John Cronin at work on the Hudson River. "I've been the
Hudson Riverkeeper since 1982, but I've been working on the Hudson
since 1974," he tells our TV production crew from his boat in the middle
of the river. John has become a national figure in the fight to protect the
Hudson River. "This section of the Hudson that we're in right now is not
only one of the most beautiful sections of the river but it's one of the most
historic sections of the river. As you travel through this part of the
Hudson, you're traveling along these jagged mountain cliffs, the old
rugged Hudson Highlands, and you're looking at them almost the same

way that the Native Americans saw them, the same way the colonists saw them. There's that great sense that taking a trip along the Hudson is taking a trip through American history."

Shortly after the train passes the town of Irvington, look to the right for a glimpse of Sunnyside, the home of Washington Irving, creator of the much loved short stories "Rip Van Winkle" and "The Legend of Sleepy Hollow." America's first internationally recognized author, Irving lived at Sunnyside from 1835 until his death in 1859. He is buried in the nearby village of Tarrytown at one of the oldest cemeteries in the country, and the rumor is that its gravestones inspired Irving's names for characters in his stories. Irving was not initially pleased to have the railroad run so close to his cottage, but he eventually became one of its better passengers. Visitors to Sunnyside can stand on the porch and watch trains pass along the banks of the Hudson River just fifty yards away, imagining what life might have been like 150 years ago at this idyllic spot. Through the eyes of Rip Van Winkle before he started his twenty-year nap, Irving provided one of literature's finest descriptions of the Hudson River Valley: "He saw at a distance the lordly Hudson, far, far below him, moving on its silent majestic course, with the reflection of a purple cloud, or the sail of a lagging bark here and there sleeping on its glassy bosom, and at last losing itself in the blue highlands."

The remnants of Bannerman Castle create one of the most romantically evocative images along the route of the Adirondack.

Sunnyside, the home of Washington Irving

The highest mountains along the Hudson River are found in the Hudson Highlands, a fifteen-mile stretch that hasn't changed much since Henry Hudson first sailed it in 1609.

The *Adirondack*'s stop at Croton-Harmon can be your gateway to "Sleepy Hollow Country," an expanse of the Hudson River Valley that includes Irving's Sunnyside as well as several other of the country's most gracious historic estates. In a ten-mile stretch near and north of Tarrytown, many of society's elite made their homes amid the lush woodlands and hills of the Hudson River Valley. Much of this part of the Hudson River retains the feel of its eighteenth- and nineteenth-century influences. The *Adirondack* arrives here in mid-morning, allowing you the option of a nearly full day of sight-seeing and an overnight stay before rejoining the next train the following morning.

The *Adirondack* pulls out of the station at Croton-Harmon into a dramatic section of the Hudson Highlands. Across the river, you can see Dunderberg Mountain, Dutch for "Thunder Mountain," and Highland Falls spilling over the cliffs. The Highlands have been called the most beautiful stretch of river scenery in the United States. It is one of the few places where the Appalachian Mountain chain is broken by a river, creating dramatic surroundings. Here the tracks pass under Bear Mountain Bridge, which carries both cars and hikers as New York State's Route 6 and the Appalachian Trail cross the Hudson River. Somewhat north of the bridge on a high hill on the west side of the Hudson is West Point, the oldest military academy in the nation. During the Revolutionary War, George Washington considered this high ground above the river the most important strategic position in the colonies, the "key to America."

As the river narrows, the landscape becomes more imposing with giant hills looming over the tracks. Storm King Mountain, at the northern end of the Hudson Highlands, is one of the most striking of the river valley's natural wonders. The train provides an excellent way to see this giant mound of granite rising above the opposite bank of the river. Soon the Breakneck

Mountains climb above the tracks as the *Adirondack* passes the attractive river village of Cold Spring and then goes through the Breakneck Ridge Tunnel. "That's Bannerman Arsenal," says conductor Rick Palmer as passengers cast bewildered looks at the strange structure on tiny Pollopel

Bannerman Castle

Island. "It was built at the turn of the century by Francis Bannerman." Bannerman built the castle, complete with a moat and drawbridge, both as a summer retreat for his family and an arsenal for his weapons business. A fire destroyed most of the buildings, leaving only the romantic remnants of a Scottish castle rising in the middle of the Hudson.

As the *Adirondack* continues north in the late morning, it enters another section of the route that is rich in American history and architecture. The train passes near Springwood, the home of Franklin D. Roosevelt, and the Vanderbilt Mansion, perhaps the grandest of all of the homes on the

A TOUR OF TARRYTOWN'S GREAT ESTATES

Philipsburg Manor

Passengers on the Adirondack *who leave the train at the Croton-Harmon stop have the opportunity to explore some of the nation's loveliest architectural treasures. First stop on the tour is Lyndhurst, one of America's finest Gothic Revival mansions and one of the best examples of a nineteenth-century estate landscape. William Paulding, a former mayor of New York City, commissioned the house in 1838, and railroad magnate Jay Gould purchased the estate as his summer home in 1880. A tour of the interior of Lyndhurst is like stepping into another time, and its dining room is known as one of the finest examples of Gothic interior design in America.*

North of Tarrytown, Philipsburg Manor is an eighteenth-century trading center complete with an operating gristmill. The estate's collection of seventeenth- and eighteenth-century Dutch, English, and colonial American furnishings and household objects is one of the finest in the nation.

Another majestic home, Van Cortland Manor, is restored to the period of the late eighteenth and early nineteenth century. Occupied for nearly 250 years by generations of the same family, it includes their collections of fine furniture, portraits, and Chinese porcelain.

The highlight of this architectural tour is Kykuit, the country house of the Rockefeller family, built between 1907 and 1913 on a hilltop in North Tarrytown with commanding views of the Hudson River and the Palisades. "Kykuit is actually one of the last of the great Hudson River estates," says Henry Joyce, project director there. "We're seeing the landscape today just as it was in 1900." Kykuit was home to four generations of Rockefellers, beginning with John D. Rockefeller, the founder of Standard Oil Company, and including Nelson Rockefeller, the four-time governor of New York and later vice president of the United States. Its landscaped terraces, formal gardens, and exceptional collection of modern sculpture create one of the great domestic landscapes in America. "The house was built here because John D. Rockefeller moved the offices of Standard Oil to New York in the early 1880s and wanted a country house outside the city," says Joyce. "The train was used a lot. We still have the carriages in the coach house that were used to collect people at the railway station."

Kykuit, the Rockefeller family's summer estate.

Hudson River. The train no longer stops at the famous Hyde Park Station, but this depot nonetheless remains an important part of rail history. "The Hyde Park Station is situated between the Roosevelt estate and the Vanderbilt estate," says Michael Rourke, a science teacher and rail fan from Kingston, New York. He helped the Hudson River Valley Railroad Society save the Hyde Park Station. "Both the Roosevelts and Vanderbilts had their own private platforms and rarely used the station," he says. "It was used once when FDR was president for the departure of the king and queen of England when they had visited the Roosevelts at Hyde Park." After extensive restoration, the Railroad Society reopened the Hyde Park Station, and today visitors can tour the old depot and soak up some history during the summer months.

Entering the Breakneck Ridge Tunnel.

Fountain at Kykuit

BRIAN SOLOMON

The Amtrak station at Rhinecliff is a starting point for exploring the historical town of Rhinebeck.

Around 11:30 A.M., the *Adirondack* arrives at the station at Rhinecliff, which can serve as the jumping-off point, so to speak, for those interested in touring this area and the Roosevelt homes at Hyde Park. Val-Kill, Eleanor Roosevelt's Hyde Park retreat, is a popular stop not far from the station, but the nearby village of Rhinebeck has one of the nation's largest collections of historic homes. The Delameter House is a classic example of an American Gothic design, and the Beekman Arms, established in 1766, claims to be America's oldest continuously operating inn. It was a favorite of FDR, and George Washington apparently really did sleep there. A little farther north, Montgomery Place, set amid 434 acres of rolling lawns, woodlands, and gardens, is one of the most significant and meticulously preserved country estates in America.

Leaving Rhinecliff around midday, the *Adirondack* passes through a marshy area that is home to many birds. Across the river, the Saugerties Lighthouse once marked the channel at the busy Esopus River. Completely restored, the lighthouse now operates as a year-round bed-and-breakfast. Before long, the *Adirondack* makes a regular stop at the town of Hudson and then a longer stopover at Albany, capital of the state and the gateway to the metropolitan area. Once it leaves the city, the train crosses the Hudson River and continues north to the town of Saratoga Springs.

The quintessential nineteenth-century American resort for the wealthy, Saratoga Springs attracted the social elite from around the country. People came to "take the waters" at the "Queen of the Spas," but their needs soon went beyond the bubbling hot springs. "Saratoga really attracted the wealthy," says Michael Venuti, park manager of the Saratoga Spa State Park. "People came to really value the

water that was here, and then it became more of a social event. While enjoying the curative powers of the water," Michael says, "people would listen to

an orchestra in the background." It
wasn't long before a gambling casi-
no and horse-racing track became
part of the Saratoga social scene.

Although Saratoga Springs is
no longer the favored getaway of the
elite, it retains many charms of a
fascinating summer resort. Actor

David Hyde-Pierce, known for his role as Niles Crane on the television series
Frasier, grew up in Saratoga Springs. He returned to his hometown to talk
about Saratoga Springs as part of the public television documentary on the
Adirondack. "I think if you get off the train, you have to get off at Saratoga,"
he says. "It's unmissable because it's such a unique combination of things. It
was formed as a spa resort and still has that element. You can go and do that.

*Actor David Hyde-Pierce grew up
in Saratoga Springs.*

Certainly go to the races if it's racing season." In Saratoga, it is easy to go from the hall of springs to the sport of kings. Even Saratoga's name evokes images of the elegant gentility surrounding the thrill and majesty of thoroughbred horse racing. The oldest racetrack in the country, it is the centerpiece of a whirl of summertime social activities. "Horse racing is a kind of unique sport," says David Hyde-Pierce. "Not a lot of places have horse racing but, more importantly, there aren't a lot of places where the tradition of horse rac-

Bear Mountain Bridge provides easy access to the United States Military Academy at West Point.

The Lake Champlain shoreline.

ing goes back as far as it does here. That culture is part of the city, and you feel it everywhere."

The *Adirondack* leaves Saratoga Springs and crosses back to the east side of the Hudson before the tracks separate from the river that has colored your journey to this point.

Now the landscape begins to change as you enter the foothills of the Adirondacks. At Fort Edwards, a series of locks was built in 1825 to connect Lake Champlain to the Hudson River and open a waterway from the St. Lawrence River to New York City. The old station at Fort Edwards serves as Amtrak's access to the Glens Falls and the Lake George recreational area. You might plan a visit to coincide with the Adirondack Balloon Festival held annually in September in Glens Falls. One of the largest such festivals in the country, it attracts more than a hundred hot-air balloonists and thousands of spectators to these southern foothills.

Not far from Glens Falls, the train enters the peaceful countryside of its namesake, the Adirondack Mountains. For the next 85 miles, the tracks trace the eastern border of Adirondack State Park, an unforgettable journey filled with serenity, beauty, and the wondrous works of nature. Encompassing more than six million acres, Adirondack Park is the largest park in the lower 48 states, bigger than Yosemite or Yellowstone. Surprisingly, less than half of the land within its boundaries is owned by the state of New York. The park is a unique mixture of public and private land. Gary Randorf is the executive director of the Adirondack Council, which tracks land-use regulations within the park. An avid outdoorsman and a landscape and nature photographer, Randorf has lived in the

Fort Ticonderoga

Adirondacks for more than twenty-five years. "There is every type of outdoor recreation you can think of here," he says. "The wilderness is so accessible. That's the big difference between the Adirondacks and some of the national parks in the west. Here, you just drive to a trailhead and park your car and step into the woods, and you're in the wilderness in moments. You'll have a sense that you're hundreds of miles away from civilization, and yet you're not." It is a very attractive landscape, and one of the best ways to see it is to ride the train." Within easy view of the tracks are many

Port Henry, home of "Champ"

opportunities to observe the remote beauty of the Adirondack wilderness.

For about the next half hour, the countryside changes as the *Adirondack* travels from the Hudson River Valley into the Champlain Valley, past dairy farms and through forests. Around two o'clock the *Adirondack* makes its regular stop at Whitehall, at the southern end of Lake Champlain. Often called the unofficial birthplace of the U.S. Navy, it was here that in 1776 Benedict Arnold formed America's first fleet, only to lose at the Battle of Valcour Bay. When the train leaves Whitehall, the rock cliffs of the Champlain Canal foreshadow the even more spectacular scenery that lies ahead. In no time at all, the train crosses South Bay to reveal the first views of Lake Champlain. "Ladies and gentlemen, the body of water next to us is Lake Champlain—122 miles of it—the sixth largest lake in the United States and the largest lake outside of the Great Lakes," conductor Craig Allyn informs the *Adirondack*'s passengers. Out the windows of the right side of the train as the *Adirondack* follows the shoreline to Montreal are the manicured farmlands and the Green Mountains of Vermont on the far side of the water.

America's early history is very much alive along this stretch of the tracks. If you hear the sound of cannon or rifle fire, it may not necessarily be your overactive imagination. During the summer months, costumed soldiers march on the grounds of Fort Ticonderoga and occasionally fire weapons. As the *Adirondack* travels up the shoreline, you may catch your first good view of Fort Ticonderoga to the right on a high peninsula jutting into the lake. Before long, the train goes into a short tunnel, built beneath the fortifications so as not to disturb the hallowed grounds of the fort, and emerges at Amtrak's small, modern station.

If you decide to get off the *Adirondack* at this stop, you won't be alone—Fort Ticonderoga is one of the most popular attractions along the rail line at the southern end of the lake. A star-shaped fortress, Ticonderoga was one in a series of strategically placed eighteenth-century military sites that command Lake Champlain. At the heart of the struggle for control of North America, Fort Ticonderoga was originally built in 1755 by the French to block the British from taking control of Lake Champlain during the Seven Years' War. It was reconstructed in 1908 and is today a gateway attraction of the Adirondacks.

North of Ticonderoga, the train continues along the rocky shoreline of Lake Champlain, which narrows dramatically at Crown Point. The *Adirondack* no longer makes a regular stop at Port Henry, the unofficial home of Champ, Lake Champlain's very own sea monster, but you may want to keep your eyes on the water as you pass. Explorer Samuel de Champlain is believed to have been the first to spot Champ, in 1609 when

Mirror Lake is one of more than 2,800 lakes and ponds that dot the Adirondack Mountains.

Champlain was mapping the southern end of the lake. Since then there have been numerous random sightings. One of those who have seen Champ is Terri Waite. She says she has spotted the legendary creature several

Saranac Lake

times, first at age thirteen and again while she was being interviewed by the *Today Show*. Nearly all of the Champ sightings have been in the Port Henry area, leading some to believe there is just a little tourism marketing keeping the legend alive. But you never know. "My recommendation," Terri says, "would be when you take a train trip through this area, look towards the water and bring your camera."

After passing Port Henry, the *Adirondack* stops at the scenic shoreline village of Westport, a good place to begin any exploration of northern Adirondack Park, including Lake Placid and Saranac Lake. Amtrak provides motorcoach connections between Westport and Lake Placid. Even with so much spectacular scenery visible from the train, you must disembark if you are to truly capture the Adirondack experience.

At the turn of the century, some of the wealthiest families in America flocked to the Adirondack lakes region and built the Great Camps of the

Charlie Ritchie

Adirondacks. More than just summer cottages, these remarkable private estates afforded the affluent every comfort imaginable in the wilds of the Adirondacks. For the public television documentary, Charlie and Mary Anne Ritchie shared with us Camp Sandanona, Charlie's family retreat for more than ninety years at the north end of Upper Saranac Lake. His parents first brought Charlie to the Adirondacks when he was three weeks old, and he has

spent part of every year here ever since. "A lot of very wealthy people had gotten wise to the idea that the Adirondacks had something special going," Charlie says. "People like the Vanderbilts, J. P. Morgan, the Whitneys, and the Rockefellers all started buying large pieces of land. The whole Great Camp era started in the 1890s and continued right into the early 1930s."

Of the more than 2,800 lakes and ponds in the Adirondacks, few can match the beauty and charm of Upper Saranac Lake. The largest of the northern Adirondack lakes, it has 5,500 acres of water surface and 100 miles of shoreline, nearly forty percent of which are protected as "Forever Wild" by the New York state constitution. "I've traveled around the world a couple of times, and I've never seen any place where everything comes together the way it does here," Charlie says. "The water and the air and the trees and the smell is all part of one whole experience for many. Climbing a mountain or hiking a trail or swimming to the island or sailing a boat is just pure enjoyment. What more can you ask for?" Today some 500 camps line the water, many of them legacies of the original families. "There's something for everybody here. You can have a really old-fashioned Adirondack experience in this particular corner of the world where nothing really has changed."

Only a few of the historic Great Camps on Upper Saranac Lake are opened to the public. The spectacular camp built by William Avery Rockefeller in the 1930s is now called The Point and is considered one of the most luxurious wilderness getaways in the country. The Wawbeek, the only year-round resort on the Upper Saranac, is a wonderful place to visit if you are looking for a few days of total serenity. If you are short on time or funds, you can capture a sense of these millionaires' getaways at the Adirondack Museum, overlooking Blue Mountain Lake. Adirondack furniture, guide boats, and more than twenty buildings of history and art are here to explore.

Back on board the *Adirondack* as it leaves Westport, high mountains rise to the left of the train while the waters of Lake Champlain narrow to the right. Nearing Willsboro, the train crosses the lovely Boquet River, where herons can often be seen. This area of the lake is known for its trout and salmon fishing. Between here and the Canadian border, the scenery becomes even more glorious than before as the *Adirondack* hugs tracks that have been carved out of the rugged cliffs along the lake. The most spectacular scenery of the journey is revealed as the train twists and

An early railroad brochure touts the splendors of vacationing in upstate New York.

COLLECTION OF BRAD S. LOMAZZI

turns on an amazing stretch of tracks along Wickham Marsh. During this five-mile section, the train makes more than 100 curves, each revealing another astounding view of the lake. "Willsboro Bay would be the highlight of the trip," says conductor Craig Allyn. "When you overlook Lake Champlain, it's breathtaking. Once you get above Whitehall, the scenery just

seems to escalate as you go higher." The son and grandson of railroad engineers, Craig has worked on the trains for more than twenty-five years. He enjoys spending time with both his regular passengers and those taking the train for the first time. "There really is no time of the year when it is more beautiful than another time. [At] Port Henry in the wintertime, when they've got the

A cabin at The Point, a luxurious camp on Upper Saranac Lake

ice fishermen out with their huts—there are hundreds of them out there. The wintertime is just a winter wonderland," Craig says before recalling the glory of autumn and, in fact, all the rest of the year. As you travel this passage, you'll no doubt share his view that no time is a bad time to enjoy one of the top ten scenic rail adventures in North America.

The scenic wonders continue as the train next passes the flag stop at Fort Kent. During the summer months, a ferry takes tourists from here to Burlington, Vermont, ten miles across the lake. Next the *Adirondack* crosses the Ausable River, which has its headwaters in the 5,344-foot Mount Marcy, the state's tallest mountain. Nearby is the Ausable Chasm, where centuries of flowing water have carved in stone what is referred to as "The Grand Canyon of the East." The landscape begins to change as the train approaches Plattsburgh and passes the giant Air Force base located there. As the *Adirondack* parts company with Lake Champlain, it dashes toward the Canadian border through forests and past miles of cornfields to Rouses Point, the last stop in the United States. Here U.S. Customs officials check southbound passengers.

Northbound passengers are checked by Canadian Customs when the *Adirondack* crosses the border at Cantic, Quebec. The stop is usually very brief but be sure you have proof of citizenship. After this interruption, the train enters the Richelieu River Valley, a flat, agricultural area with a spattering of small farming communities. This quaint region provides a perfect ambience for quiet reflection at the end of this rail adventure. As the Montreal skyline comes into view, the *Adirondack* crosses the St. Lawrence River on the Victoria Bridge. "Ladies and gentlemen, if I could have your attention please," says conductor Craig

The Montreal skyline from the Victoria Bridge

Allyn, making his final passenger announcement. "As you can see, we're just going over the St. Lawrence River with the skyline of Montreal off to the right, the final destination point for this evening's train. We'd like to wish you a pleasant stay in Montreal and hope you will consider Amtrak again in the near future." The lights of the city await you.

THE TRAIN:

The Sierra Madre Express, a private excursion train with a lounge car, three sleeping cars, and an observation dome/dining car.

THE ROUTE:

More than 1,300 miles, from sea level to 8,000 feet through the heart of Mexico's Sierra Madre range and the Copper Canyon, a region of rugged natural beauty including areas accessible only by rail.

DURATION OF THE TRIP:

Eight days and seven nights, including two nights in a Tucson hotel, two nights on the train, and three nights in Mexican hotels along the route.

HIGHLIGHTS:

• The exotic, rugged scenery of the Copper Canyon and a train route that includes eighty-seven tunnels and thirty-five bridges.

• The native Tarahumara Indians, known for their long-distance running, their fine basket making, and their traditional cave dwellings.

• The opportunity to visit several quaint Mexican villages.

There is really no way to prepare for the visual feast and unique cultural encounter that is the train journey through

MEXICO'S

COPPER

THIS REGION OF THE SIERRA TARAHUMARA RANGE contains one of the world's largest clusters of giant canyons, and wild, untouched natural beauty is the main attraction here. Cloud-topped mountain peaks, plunging gorges, cascading waterfalls, and an amazing array of flowering plants and towering trees add to the splendor of the chasms themselves.

This remote, largely untrammeled wilderness is also home to 50,000 reclusive Tarahumara Indians. The isolation of this area has helped the Tarahumara preserve their culture perhaps better than any native group in North America. Along the rail journey, you'll encounter the Tarahumara and get a broad understanding of their culture and the challenging life they lead within these mountains. As the train snakes along the rims of deep canyons through the heart of Tarahumara territory, this rail journey slowly reveals the secrets of the *barrancas*—the canyons.

The combination of the incredible scenery, the remoteness of the area traversed by the train, and the opportunity to learn about the Tarahumara and Mexican cultures is what makes the Copper Canyon such an exceptional rail journey experience. Roberto Balderrama, owner of several hotels along the train route, says, "You have to see it. It's another world. You have the beauty, the romance, and the adventure—it's all part of the trip to Copper Canyon."

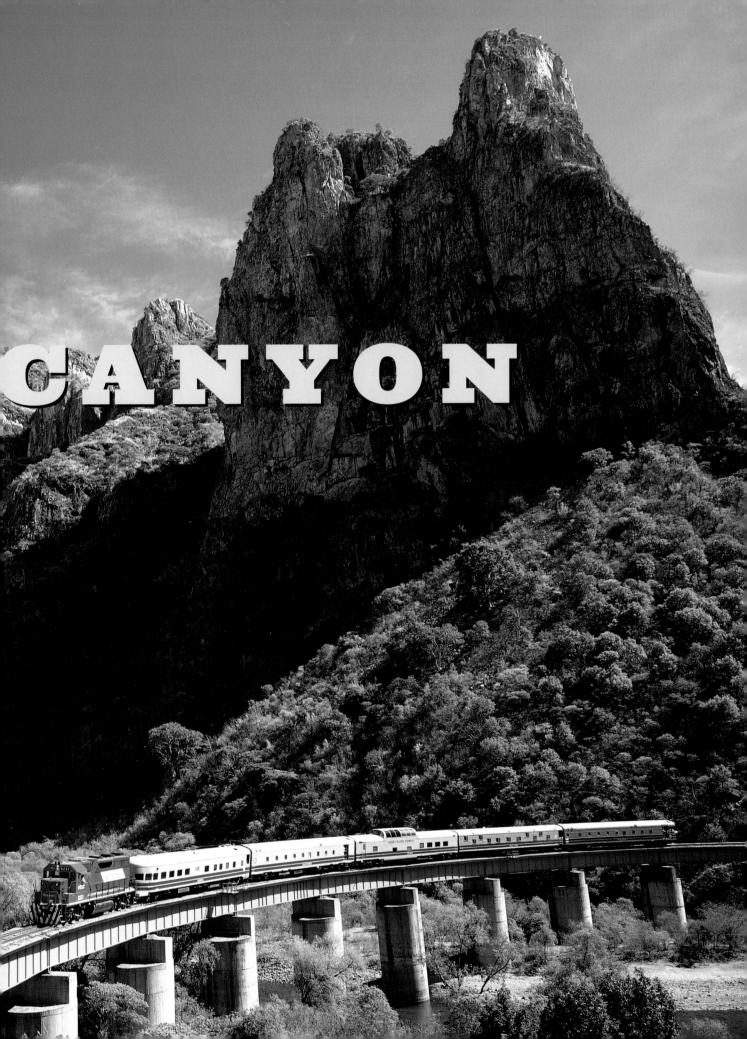

CANYON

Roberto Balderrama

Much of what we expect of Mexico is defined by our limited exposure to Mexican life and landscapes. For many, Mexico is either a bustling, often intimidating border town or an isolated beach resort along Mexico's golden coast. We take a day trip over the border to Tijuana or Nogales, and that's usually enough to satisfy our curiosity. Or we pack a bag and head for Mexico's Riviera, lured by visions of surf and hot sands etched in our imaginations by movies and vacation ads. Neither of these experiences typically provides much of a sense of the real Mexico or the Mexican people. That is not true of a visit to the Copper Canyon. "You have to take the train to come to the Copper Canyon," says hotelier Balderrama. "We don't have beaches. We don't have tennis or golf. This is a different kind of vacation." Señor Balderrama has some simple advice for visitors: "Take it easy a little bit, especially in the canyons where life goes on for centuries without change."

Traveling by rail into the Barranca del Cobre, as the Copper Canyon is known in Mexico, quickly takes visitors well beyond the stereotypical tourist jaunts. Here the adventurous find another, largely unexplored Mexico. It is the land of the Sierra Madre Occidental range, the area featured in the classic American movie, *Treasure of the Sierra Madre,* starring Humphrey Bogart. "Beyond that river, the country's very wild and dangerous," Bogart is warned by an old prospector. While the territory is less intimidating today, it remains a rough, exotic wilderness. Along the railroad tracks are places that look like scenes from an old western movie. "This is pretty wild country," says Peter Robbins, who operates a private rail company that provides access to the Copper Canyon. "You can go 100 yards off the side of the tracks and go places where white people haven't gone. Period."

Defining Copper Canyon can be confusing. The Barranca del Cobre is actually made up of several intersecting canyons, and the term "Copper Canyon" generally refers to three different geographic areas. In the narrowest sense, Copper Canyon is a specific copper mine near the village of Tejaban, but the name also applies to a specific canyon that begins at the Humira Bridge and ends just above the mining town of Urique. The term is also used generically to describe the total canyon system in the Mexican state of Chihauhua. An area of 25,000 square miles, it is the largest canyon system in North America.

Without the railroad, much of this place would be inaccessible. At the heart of the Copper Canyon experience is the famed rail line that runs between Los Mochis and Chihuahua. Known as the Chihuahua al Pacifico Railway, this rail line is acclaimed as an engineering miracle, traversing 400 miles from sea level to an altitude of 8,000 feet through some of Mexico's most majestic mountain country. The railway wasn't built as a tourist route; that concept was unheard of during the time the track was laid from the 1880s to the 1960s. The Chihuahua al Pacifico rail line was a commercial venture, designed to shorten the distance between Kansas City and the Pacific Ocean—that is, to bring the products of the American Midwest more quickly to Asian markets.

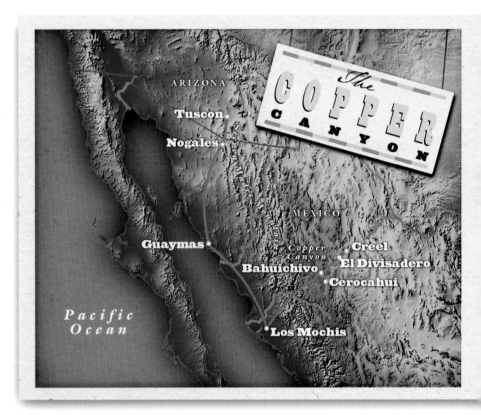

Now the route carries more passengers than products, but still only a few options exist for reaching the Copper Canyon by train.

Until recently, the Mexican government operated the trains along the Chihuahua al Pacifico route. Since the railroad system in Mexico was privatized, the Ferrocarril Mexicano company—known locally as Ferro Mex—has offered daily trips through the Copper Canyon. These regularly scheduled rides provide a reasonably priced way for independent travelers to visit the area at their own pace, planning their own itineraries. Most American tourists, however, take one of several excursion trains that provide fully packaged tours to the Copper Canyon.

For the public television documentary, we boarded Peter Robbins' *Sierra Madre Express*. Based in Tucson, Arizona, it offers an eight-day, seven-night trip thirty times a year, plus a special New Year's trip. Two-thirds of the trips are operated by Tauck Tours and follow a slightly different itinerary than the route we took. (The colonial cities of El Fuerta and Alamos are included in those excursions.) For the trip we filmed, passengers must make their own way, by whatever means they choose, to Tucson, the starting and ending points for the *Sierra Madre Express* journeys. After an overnight stay at a Tucson hotel, you take a bus to the train station at Nogales, Mexico, and board the *Sierra Madre Express* for a welcome reception.

Passengers toast the end of their first day onboard the Sierra Madre Express.

The *Sierra Madre Express* consists of five refurbished passenger cars, including a selection of sleeping accommodations. The interior design is casually comfortable rather than formal, an approach that puts passengers at ease immediately. All food, water, and ice are brought on board from the United States. Locomotives run by Ferro Mex crews pull the *Sierra Madre Express* cars and the train's Mexican staff works hand in hand with the American train staff to ensure the safety and comfort of each voyager. In 1998 the American Society of Travel Writers voted the *Sierra Madre Express* "the world's most exciting train ride."

As the train pulls out of Nogales in the late afternoon, the scenery is ordinary. Certainly nothing outside the windows foreshadows the magnificent vistas that lie ahead. Nonetheless, joy soon overtakes you. You are on board a train bound for a mysterious, little-known destination. For Peter Robbins of the *Sierra Madre Express,* this first leg of the journey is, in fact, a vital part of the adventure. "If you simply fly into Mexico on an airplane and get up at four o'clock in the morning to make a six o'clock train to go see the canyon, you're upset, you're not down to speed," he says. "On our particular trip, traveling 400 miles south takes twenty-four hours, and it gives everybody a chance to slow down, relax, and get ready to see Mexico."

The slowing down is not a problem. After dinner, you have time to explore the train and meet fellow passengers before turning in for the night. Staterooms vary in size and configuration. Most are small, but they're perfectly comfortable for the few nights you sleep on the train. Each room has a

THE SIERRA MADRE EXPRESS

"It's a very special little train," says its owner Peter Robbins and, for those interested in rail history, it has a lot to offer. "It will never be a great big commercial operation," he continues "and I think that's kind of the joy in how the Sierra Madre operates. We mortgaged everything we owned to get some money for the first trips. As the years went by, we would add and build one car and then it would be a three-car train, and then it was a four-car train. Little by little, it has grown."

Peter Robbins

Now the Sierra Madre Express typically runs a five-car train into the Copper Canyon, and all of the beautifully restored coaches have a special charm. The most popular car, especially attractive to photographers and bird-watchers, is the "Divisadero" with its open-air lounge and observation area. Originally built in 1949 for the Union Pacific Railroad, it provides room for about twenty passengers to gather on its open-air observation deck—a spectacular place to enjoy the beauty and spirit of the trip. "You can smell Mexico. You can hear Mexico," says Peter Robbins with his typical enthusiasm for both the country and the train. "You're actually participating in the sights, sounds, and smells of Mexico." The "Arizona" is a lounge car with a glass-enclosed observation area. Built in 1946 by the Pullman Company, it originally ran on the Northern Pacific between Chicago and Seattle. Retired from service in the mid-1950s, it has been refurbished to its original state. The Sierra Madre Express also has a dome car that offers unrestricted views of the terrain. Plenty of wide windows and comfortable seats in every car allow for the primary activity of this trip—soaking up the passing scenery.

The Chihuahua al Pacifico rail line is a journey through contrasting landscapes and changing climates. The line serves as an important link for remote Mexican villages to the outside world.

©KERRICK JAMES

sink and toilet but no shower. If you've traveled by train before, you already know one of the basic rules: Pack light. There isn't a lot of storage space in your compartment.

Traveling through the night, the *Sierra Madre Express* heads toward the Copper Canyon, traversing the Sonoran Desert and skirting the Sea of Cortez. While you're sleeping, the train passes Hermosillo, one of Sonora's major industrial towns, and Ciudad Obregón, one of Mexico's largest agricultural centers. You may notice salt air and sea breezes as the train passes Empalme and the port of Guaymas. Twenty miles to the west is the resort of

San Carlos, home to one of Mexico's Club Med resorts.

Just after dawn the *Sierra Madre Express* turns northeast into the Copper Canyon. Morning on the train brings a cornucopia of sights, sounds, smells, and experiences. The Mexican spirit of *compañero,* or comradeship, evolves as travelers discuss the coming days over the aromas of coffee and a delicious breakfast. You have left far behind the television, cell phones, faxes, and e-mail that clutter everyday life. "If you slow down enough," explains Peter Robbins, "what you do on this trip, because of the nature of being on the train, is you begin to relate to the Indians and to the tranquility that still resides here." Robbins founded Rail Passenger Services, Inc., the parent company of the *Sierra Madre Express,* in 1979 and began the first train tours into the Copper Canyon in 1987. "One of the

things we have in short supply in our busy world is tranquility," he says. "Down here we move at a slightly different pace. You're also getting great views, but you're getting the tranquility and the peace you can find in these mountains." During the morning the *Sierra Madre Express* climbs steadily through the western foothills of the Sierra Madre Occidental into the Sierra Tarahumara.

The Chihuahua al Pacifico rail line is a marvel of persistence, design, and construction skill. Within a stretch of a few miles you begin to experience the wonders of its engineering and construction.

Located in the Sierra Madre Occidental mountain range, the Barranca del Cobre, or Copper Canyon, is actually a series of gorges, some deeper than the Grand Canyon.

The Sierra Madre Express passes through the lush Mexican countryside.

Crossing El Fuerte Bridge

First you encounter the magnificent bridge over the Rio Fuerte. At 1,637 feet, it is the longest on the railroad. If you glance over the side, you'll see the remnants of a freight train that tried to cross the bridge a little too fast. Next the train enters the first of eighty-seven tunnels that are carved

The 1,000-foot-long Rio Chinipas Bridge

through the mountains along the route. El Descanso, the first of five tunnels in a row, is the longest on the entire journey. The train takes nearly two minutes to travel its inky 5,996-foot span. The train then crosses the 1,000-foot-long bridge spanning the Rio Chinipas. At 335 feet, this is the highest of the thirty-five bridges on the railway. Looking down as the train inches slowly across the bridge, you see nothing but water, as the train seems to float in midair. Out the right side, below the rail bridge, you can spot a suspension bridge for foot and burro traffic. Also hundreds of feet above the water, it is appropriately called the "Chinipas Walking Bridge." No doubt you feel very glad to be crossing in the comfort and safety of the train.

The beautiful Santa Barbara Bridge

Soon the train crosses another bridge and then passes through more tunnels before emerging into the truly mountainous terrain of canyon country. Here the high climb begins as the canyon steepens. Grades range from 2.3% to 2.5%. Most of the boxcars you see parked along the tracks are former World War II troop cars that are now homes for the railroad workers. During this daylong climb through the mountains, you enjoy a relaxing lunch served right at your seat to ensure that you don't miss any of the passing scenery.

As the train parallels the course of the Rio Septentrion, it enters the steepest part of the canyon. Here the desert vegetation gives way to lush woodland. You may notice palm, banana, and even mango trees along this section of the route. In this most beautiful stretch of the journey, the train is virtually hemmed in by the rising canyon walls. "Another bridge coming up," observes a passenger. "It's the Santa Barbara Bridge, 714 feet." Using the helpful milepost guides provided by the *Sierra Madre Express,* another passenger alerts fellow travelers to one of the engineering highlights of the route. "This is tunnel 50 we're going through," she says. "That's our last tunnel before we approach Temoris."

Of the many engineering feats on this route, the most amazing are the bridges, tunnels, and loops at Temoris. The train crosses the exquisite Santa Barbara Bridge, passes the village of Temoris, climbs through a great loop up the western canyon wall, and enters a long tunnel. Steep rock faces made the construction of conventional switchbacks impossible. Instead, a 3,074-foot tunnel makes a 180-degree turn inside the mountain. When the train emerges some seventy seconds later, it is headed in the opposite direction and still climbing. You can peer down at the three levels of track the train has just traversed. It is a staggering achievement of railroad engineering and construction. At this location on November 23, 1961, the Chihuahua al Pacifico railroad line was dedicated. A huge metal sign, constructed of rails 22 feet long with letters 2 feet high, commemorates the completion.

A change in the environment is evident as the train emerges from the last tunnel at Temoris. The air freshens, and the vegetation of the upper canyon changes to fragrant pine and hardwood forests. At nearly a mile above sea level, the train passes Bahuichivo. On the return trip in a few days, the train stops at Bahuichivo, and passengers will spend a night at a nearby Mexican village. This area is noted for its production of apples, and you can see the orchards in the valley and on the slopes. In a relatively short stretch of track, the train crosses four bridges, each one roughly 400 feet long. Along this stretch, you see stunning views of great jagged peaks and deep river gorges.

Crossing La Laja Bridge.

As the train pushes deeper into canyon country, the magnificence of the views and the wild ruggedness of the terrain are breathtaking. The canyon is narrow and maze-like at this point, with sheer rock walls. La Laja Bridge, at 695 feet, is the second highest on the route and is followed immediately by a tunnel, a combination that was especially tricky for the builders of the line. The train glides smoothly from tunnel to tunnel, sometimes entering a new tunnel before the entire train has exited the previous one. The dark, dank, cave-like atmosphere of the tunnels is a sharp contrast to the bright, warm air of the canyon cliffs.

THE RAILROAD THAT COULDN'T BE BUILT

The rugged landscape of Copper Canyon that attracts visitors today was a major obstacle to building the Chihuahua al Pacifico railroad. Built during revolutions and in spite of bankruptcies, the line took more than ninety years to build at a cost of over $100 million. The 560-mile-long rail line from the Texas border to the Pacific Ocean wasn't completed until 1961, when this magnificent region was finally opened to the casual traveler.

Passing through one of the most spectacular rock impediments on the route.

Early railroads in this area supported the traffic from mines, cattle, agriculture, and timber. But it wasn't until 1872 that Albert Owen, an idealistic civil engineer from Chester, Pennsylvania, envisioned building a rail line through the Copper Canyon. Owen's dream was to shorten the distance between Kansas City and the Pacific Ocean, thus getting American goods to Asian markets quicker and cheaper. This was before the Panama Canal existed, and only one transcontinental railroad across the United States had been completed.

In 1881 Owen received permission from the Mexican government to build the railroad. After some initial success with the construction on the level areas near Los Mochis and Chihuahua, construction approached the rugged Sierra Madre mountains. The seemingly impassable mountains, combined with his illness and disillusionment, caused Owen to abandon the project in 1893.

ELADIO RAMOS PIÑA

The Chihuahua al Pacifico Railway was built through some of the most rugged terrain in North America. Tarahumara natives made up much of the workforce.

In 1900 American railroad tycoon Edward Arthur Stilwell was next to try the impossible. One of Stilwell's construction contractors was the legendary Pancho Villa. During the Mexican Revolution, Villa the rail builder became Villa the scourge of the railroad, tearing up sections of his own work to disrupt government troops.

The Mexican government took over the project in the 1940s, but it would be another twenty years before the final section of track was completed. All of the engineering and construction expertise that could be found was required to finish the two most difficult sections of the railroad. The first of these were the loops at Temoris, which reverse the direction of the train's ascent to allow it to climb the mountain. The second feat occurred near the station of Pitorreal, where the train actually circles back on itself with a complete loop, one of only three examples of this type of railway construction found in North America.

Of the 2,000 to 3,000 workers who built the railroad, most were Tarahumara Indians. "It was extremely dangerous work," says Peter Robbins of the Sierra Madre Express. "A lot of people were killed building the tunnels. There would be unexpected landslides and cave-ins inside the tunnels." During most of the construction, workers made do with very limited tools. Hand tools, such as picks, shovels, crowbars, and sledges were the most common devices. Explosives helped during the early years, but heavy equipment was mostly unavailable until the final years of construction.

Finally on November 23, 1961, the president of Mexico, with official guests from all over the world, opened the new section and created the first "easy" access into the heart of the Copper Canyon region. Often called "the marvel of Mexico," more than a half-million passengers a year travel through the Copper Canyon region on these historic train tracks.

The most difficult construction occurred in the 1950s along some 160 miles of track across the Sierra Occidental range.

The combined length of the eighty-eight tunnels along the route is almost fourteen miles.

Tarahumara natives often travel long distances to sell their handmade pots, baskets, dolls, and other native crafts to tourists at Divisadero.

As you arrive at Divisadero around mid-afternoon, the first full day on the train draws to an end. Passengers have been on board the *Sierra Madre Express* for nearly twenty-four hours, yet no one seems restless. As Peter Robbins predicted, most are now down to speed, and very few seem anxious to leave the train and the non-stop scenic wonders. It has been an exhilarating day, passing through some of the most incredible scenery that can be enjoyed from a train anywhere in the world.

After the narrow gorges and sheer cliffs that characterized the day's journey, Divisadero provides an opportunity for wide views of the canyons and the first dazzling vista of the Barranca del Cobre from its rim. Indeed, *El Divisadero* means "the view." Divisadero–Barranca del Cobre actually provides a panorama of three giant canyons: The Copper, the Tararecua, and the Urique can be seen from here. Since early times, the Tarahumara have come here to commune with nature. According to their tradition, the Great Spirit put the wonders of nature here for their eyes to enjoy. The canyons are among the greatest expressions of His love for them. At 7,700 feet above the canyon floor, Divisadero is the highest accessible point on the train route. The view leaves a lasting, spiritual, and almost overwhelming impression.

Divisadero also provides a first encounter with the Tarahumara Indians. The Tarahumara create a makeshift bazaar at the Divisadero Station to sell

©KERRICK JAMES

Built on the rim of the canyon, the thirty-seven-room Posada Barrancas Mirador Hotel provides luxury accommodations near Divisadero.

their wares, including an array of beautiful handmade items. Passengers wander through the booths and stretch their legs before heading to the hotel. It is a delightful experience to see the colorfully dressed Tarahumara women with their handcrafted baskets woven from native grasses and pine needles. Many of the basket makers hike long distances from the depths of the canyon to sell their work. They arrive just before the train and leave soon after it departs, only to repeat the cycle again the next day. Some tourists feel the urge

to negotiate with the natives on the cost of their unpriced items. Regardless of the sales of their popular goods, however, most natives live in virtual poverty. An extra dollar or two for a finely crafted gift certainly means a great deal to a Tarahumara family.

Roberto Balderrama

Divisadero is the first off-train overnight stop for the *Sierra Madre Express*. You spend two nights here and use this as a starting point for day trips to other parts of the canyon. The Posada Barrancas Mirador Hotel is perched literally on the canyon rim. This modern hotel offers deluxe rooms and the gracious service that is the hallmark of a Balderrama facility. Since 1962 the Balderrama Hotel chain has pioneered the establishment of tourist hotels in the vast Copper Canyon region. Hotel owner Roberto Balderrama is an enthusiastic booster of the region. "This is a real treasure, not only for Mexico . . . for humanity," he says. "The Copper Canyon is still not developed. It's one of the last frontiers of Mexico."

Raquel Moreno

The Posada Barrancas Mirador Hotel hangs over the edge of the Copper Canyon, where the sheer drop-off is more than a mile. "When persons come here," chuckles hotel manager Raquel Moreno, "they say 'ooh' because they are right on the rim of the canyon, and you can see the canyon everywhere you stay in the hotel. Every room has a balcony to the canyon." Accommodations reflect the Tarahumara influence and the culture of the state of Chihuahua. "This hotel was built by the Tarahumara Indians who live around the canyon up those mountains," Moreno says. "We didn't use any machines. Everything is handmade. All the ornaments and the tile . . . the walls are adobe. Everything is natural. We use everything from Mexico, from this area." One of your best memories of the trip may be watching the sun set into the *barrancas* from the balcony of your room at El Mirador.

After a good night's sleep and a hearty Mexican breakfast, you reboard the *Sierra Madre Express* for a one-day excursion from Divisadero to nearby Creel. You'll return to El Mirador in time for dinner. The scenery here isn't as majestic as it was the previous day, but the pine forest, rocky hills, and green valleys make for a pleasant, relaxing two-hour train ride to Creel. Along the way, the train negotiates "El Lazo," another of the engineering achievements of the railroad. "The Loop" is one of the few places in the world where the rails actually cross over themselves. At Los Ojitos, the train crosses the Continental Divide and reaches its highest point on the rail line at 8,071 feet.

Fireplaces in each room at El Mirador help to warm the sometimes cool Mexican evenings.

Creel is a rugged logging town nestled back in the mountains away from the edge of the canyon. A fascinating mix of frontier town and tourist haven, it is populated by Tarahumara Indians, loggers, and tourists from around

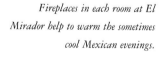

the world. It serves as a melting pot for the region's inhabitants. "We have a mix of several cultures in Creel," says Peter Robbins. "We have the Mexican culture in Creel. We have the Tarahumaras who live on the outskirts of Creel. Then we have a small Anglo community, and then we have some of the Mennonite influence because down the rails toward Chihuahua is a Mennonite community. So occasionally in Creel, you'll hear German spoken, which is kind of unique." Creel is an excellent jumping-off point for trips deeper into the canyon, including an opportunity to more closely observe the unique and seldom seen culture of the Tarahumara.

Watching the sun set into the barrancas from El Mirador is a highlight of this journey.

More than 50,000 Tarahumara live in the barrancas (canyons) of Chihuahua. Many still live a traditional lifestyle in natural caves.

The Tarahumara are known for their long-distance running skills.

Pedro Palma

The Last Mexican Frontier was first discovered by Captain Francisco de Ubarra, a Spanish conquistador, in 1564. When the Spaniards arrived in the Chihuahua region, they found the Tarahumara—but not for long. The Tarahumara retreated deep into the forbidding and mysterious *barrancas,* never to be conquered or enslaved. Nevertheless, by the beginning of this century, their land had been reduced to the remote, isolated area of the Copper Canyon. "Tarahumaras are special people," says Roberto Balderrama, "different from any groups in Mexico. They are shy but friendly." While the Tarahumara benefit from the increased tourism in the Copper Canyon, they also struggle to preserve their way of life. You have to live with them to understand them," Balderrama says. "So when you go there for a few days and say 'hello' and buy some things from them, you are not really knowing the Indians," he counsels.

Today most Tarahumara live in timber or stone houses. A few still live traditionally in caves and supplement their income by opening their unusual homes to curious visitors. The best way to visit a Tarahumara cave is with a knowledgeable guide like Pedro Palma, who arranged for our television crew to visit a Tarahumara cave dwelling. Palma, who is part Indian and part Mexican, was raised by the Tarahumara. His knowledge and experience enable him to personalize these often-shy people. "There's a great story of the man who used to live here," says Palma as we approach the nearest inhabited cave home. "He passed away last December. Sebastian is how we refer to his cave—Sebastian's cave. He used to be the mailman between here and Wachochi, which is 150 kilometers from here. There wasn't a road then, and it used to take him about ten days to get there," Palma explains. "Now there are five Tarahumara living inside this cave." The Tarahumara are a proud and independent people who have clung steadfastly to their way of life. Sebastian's daughter Maria and her family live in a very traditional but slowly disappearing manner.

©KERRICK JAMES

Dressed in their typically colorful clothing, Tarahumara women weave baskets from pine needles and sotol, a plant with long thorny leaves.

The outside world knows the Tarahumara as legendary long-distance runners. The Tarahumara call themselves "Raramuri" or "Foot Runners" and have been running some of these trails through the canyons for hundreds of years. "Running is not only a sport," says Pedro Palma. "Practicing the race or kicking the wooden ball brings the community together and gives them the opportunity to practice their social life." This is essential to a group that lives scattered all over in the high Sierras and deep in the canyons. In the traditional Tarahumara race, two teams kick and chase a wooden ball over the rocky countryside. It can go on for days. "In the Tarahumara race, often the winner is whoever is standing," says Palma. "The loser will be lying somewhere along the trail."

Creel provides another excellent opportunity to purchase Tarahumara crafts. An easy walk from the train station, the Mission Store provides an outlet for native artisans to sell their crafts. Here you can find dolls, pottery, woven purses and belts, musical instruments, bead necklaces, baskets, wood carvings, wool rugs—even cassettes of Tarahumara music. All proceeds go to the Mission Hospital run by Father Luis Verplancken, a Jesuit missionary. The hospital has been a fixture in Creel since 1967, providing free care to the Tarahumara and all others who need it.

Back on the train, the short ride from Creel back to Divisadero goes quickly and is a good time to catch a relaxing nap. The second night at El Mirador includes a lavish Mexican dinner and entertainment provided by the Tarahumara—usually music and dancing or the reenactment of a traditional native race.

In the morning, light spills into the *barrancas,* revealing rivers and side canyons obscured by last night's shadows. You have the morning free for exploring the canyon area around Divisadero on your own. Some people opt

for a thrilling helicopter ride into the vast Copper Canyon. Others take a short hike into the canyon for another opportunity to visit a Tarahumara cave home. One family that often sells handmade items at El Mirador lives in a cave just below the hotel, an easy twenty-minute walk along a stone path. Tourists may be uneasy about how or even whether to approach a Tarahumara cave. After all, this is someone's home. Most of the cave-dwelling Tarahumara, especially those located near the rim of the canyon, are used to sightseers, and they allow visitors in as a way to earn a few pesos. Few of these retiring people, however, engage visitors in conversation. While you may feel slightly awkward, the opportunity to see how these reclusive natives live, almost as their ancestors did centuries ago, is worth the trip into the canyon.

Hotel El Mision at Cerocahui

Cerocahui is dominated by the distinctive red brick church that was built in 1680 by Father Juan Maria Salvatierra, a Franciscan priest and the first white man to enter this area.

Following lunch at El Mirador, the *Sierra Madre Express* heads back down the canyon. As the train retraces its way through the canyons, different angles of sunlight and perspective provide fresh views of the *barrancas*. But even as the train starts toward home, the Copper Canyon adventure is not yet complete. It's about a two-hour trip south to Bahuichivo, the jumping-off point for a visit to Cerocahui, considered one of the most beautiful mountain villages in Mexico. While the distance from Bahuichivo is only about 7 miles, the bus trip to Cerocahui takes about an hour over a rough, dusty, and bone-jarring road.

Resting on a mile-high plateau, Cerocahui is in the wild frontier of northwest Mexico. The old Jesuit Mission, founded in 1680, is thought to be one of the most attractive churches in the Sierra Tarahumara. The church's gilded dome wasn't finished until 1741. Like many churches in the Sierra Madre, it fell into disrepair over the centuries, but a major reconstruction of the chapel's exterior was completed in the 1940s. Jesuits continue to conduct their mission here, including operating a boarding school for native Tarahumara children. The Tarahumara are generally so isolated that if parents want their children to be educated, they must send them to a school like this from as far away as 150 miles.

©THE PHOTOFILE/GERALD L. FRENCH

Next to the church is the Hotel El Mision, owned by Roberto Balderrama. "Cerocahui is a unique village," says Balderrama. "A real Mexican Tarahumara village dating back to 1690." Cerocahui is little changed from the time when the Jesuits swept through the area converting the Tarahumara Indians. "That little village stays for centuries the same way of living," Balderrama says. Its timeless quality is what separates Cerocahui from the rest of the towns of the Copper Canyon. Balderrama's desire to capture that experience for visitors is what led him to build a hotel at this remote location. "I decided to build a hotel here for adventurers, for tourists," he says. "They're looking for different places. The real old Mexico is in Cerocahui." The picturesque setting and pace of life make Cerocahui a special destination.

Once a grand hacienda, the Hotel El Mision has been converted into a cozy, rustic lodge with colorful Indian and colonial decor. A huge fireplace separates the hotel's lobby and dining room, a small bar serves beer and drinks, and plenty of sofas and chairs invite you to relax and mingle with the natives and other guests. The wilderness experience is enhanced by the realities of the isolation of the village. Electricity in Cerocahui is limited to a few hours each evening. After that, the town goes dark. Kerosene lamps are provided in each room, as is plenty of hot water. The hotel also has a generator that operates for an hour or so in the morning. You hardly miss the typical amenities of modern life. Cerocahui is far from civilization, yet at this charming inn no one seems to mind.

The following morning marks your last chance to explore the Copper Canyon. A bus excursion to the Cerro del Gallego lookout offers one last memorable panoramic scene. It is a sweeping view of Urique Canyon, one of the most beautiful canyons of the Sierra Madre. Both sides of Urique can be seen from this point, with the river sparkling far below. The tiny cluster of structures at the very bottom of the canyon is the old mining town of Urique.

The Cerocahui Waterfalls, or Wicochi. In Tarahumara it means "place of many fir trees."

Adventurous tourists travel by horseback to waterfalls, an abandoned gold mine, and other sites near Cerocahui.

*A river winds
along the bottom of spectacular
Urique Canyon.*

    If you are slightly more adventurous, you can forgo the bus trip and have the hotel arrange a horseback excursion to the waterfalls and other scenic and historic sites in the area. To explore the Sierra Tarahumara on horseback is to see it the way the missionaries and conquistadors saw it more than 300 years ago. The willing, if sometimes headstrong, steeds are a pleasant means of transportation through the countryside. One of the best destinations is the beautiful Wicochi Falls. In Tarahumara, *wicochi* means "place of many fir trees." The hour-long horseback ride is followed by a thirty-minute hike to the waterfall. It is definitely a trip for the more adventurous traveler, but the experience itself, as well as the beauty of the destination, are well worth the effort.

    After lunch back at the Hotel El Mision, you board the *Sierra Madre Express* for the trip back to Tucson. The rugged beauty of the Copper Canyon and the Sierra Madre recede into the distance. Your weeklong jour-

ney has provided not only a better understanding of this majestic and mysterious region but also a treasure of memories that are as colorful as the dresses of the Tarahumara women and as long lasting as the meandering of the train along the canyon rim. The true scope and scale of the Barrancas del Cobre are difficult to comprehend. No map or written description comes close to conveying the immensity of the land or the ruggedness of the terrain. This trek into the past has been a sensuous delight, stirring the mind and soothing the soul. "That's why they come here to the canyons," says Roberto Balderrama. "To relax and take it easy and enjoy the time. That's the beautiful thing of this trip," he says. "You are not rushing. You are resting. You are reading. You are talking. You are making good conversation. Enjoying life. I think this is a great thing." For those aboard the *Sierra Madre Express,* the days in the canyon come to an end, and the journey closes much as it began, with a long enchanting ride into the Mexican night.

The window of the train gliding through the Colorado Rockies looks out on slopes studded with prehistoric bones and the ghosts of settlers and gold miners chasing their westward dreams. This is

THE ROCKI

"When passengers come on this train going to the Rockies, they see some pretty dramatic scenes," says naturalist and train guide John Borneman. *"Every time they come around a corner, they don't know what they're going to see."*

THE ROCKY MOUNTAINS WERE ONCE A GREAT barrier that allowed only a trickle of civilization through to the west—until the train breached it. For more than a century, the railroad and the Rockies have challenged one another. Today, they offer an unforgettable train journey experience. "Taking a train through the Rockies opens your mind and your eyes to a vastness and contrast that you could never imagine or see in any other way," says Borneman. "It's not something that is at a distance, and that's what's really exciting about traveling on a train. You're not separated from it. The train is part of this whole environment you're going through."

ES BY RAIL

Our journey heads west on a route from Denver through the Colorado Rockies and across the Continental Divide before turning north through Utah to Salt Lake City, then into Idaho, and on to Yellowstone and Grand Teton National Parks. While there is much to see and explore at the selected stops along the way, the real payoff of this trip is the first day's journey through the Rocky Mountains. The train slithers through canyons on tracks laid seemingly on hope and through wild country that is still mostly inaccessible. Closeness and intimacy exists between the train and the surrounding landscape, an ambience that is impossible to experience any other way—except perhaps on foot. But it would take virtually a lifetime to explore on foot what we will see in a day from the train. Once you travel through this section of the Rockies by train, you'll be tempted to turn around and take this part of the trip over again.

Not only are you in for some stunning scenery on this journey, but the train is itself something special. You are traveling on a private luxury train of vintage Pullman cars called the *American Orient Express*. The *AOE* is a private rail company that offers a variety of trips throughout the United States. In fact, the company is constantly tinkering with its trip itineraries and has changed some portions of this trip since we were onboard to record "The Rockies by Rail" television program for PBS. Fifteen vintage rail cars have been completely and beautifully restored. Loaded with gourmet food and refreshments, the *AOE* attempts to re-create the train travel experience of a half-century ago—the romantic days of railroading, when many Americans got their first look at the Rockies from the window of a train. "The scenery is magical, and the train is magical," says Greg Mueller, who oversaw the restoration of the 1940s and 1950s train cars. "The *American Orient Express* experience is a step back into history, a magical reenactment of train life fifty to sixty years ago that has not been available for many years."

The beautifully restored blue and gold cars of the American Orient Express *include the New York Observation Car, which was dedicated by Dwight Eisenhower in 1948.*

AN AMTRAK ALTERNATIVE

The American Orient Express *is an exceptional way to see the Rocky Mountains from the train. Some travelers, however, may find that the AOE is too expensive or doesn't provide enough flexibility for exploration along the route. For those travelers, Amtrak's California Zephyr is a great alternative. Following the path of Western pioneers, gold prospectors, and the Pony Express, the California Zephyr is arguably Amtrak's most scenic route. The 2,400-mile journey takes three days and two nights, beginning in Chicago and ending in Oakland, California.*

In the 1940s and 1950s, the California Zephyr was considered the West's premier train. Like the gentle west wind it is named for, the California Zephyr breezed gracefully along the tracks, providing many people with their first look at the American West. It was a sleek, streamlined train with as many as five Vista-Domes, the only transcontinental train of its day to offer such cars, for spectacular viewing of the passing scenery. This historically significant train followed much of the route established with the building of America's first transcontinental railroad, still considered one of the world's greatest railroading feats. Today's Zephyr offers Superliner service that includes coach and sleeping cars, a sight-seeing lounge, and a dining car, and it features such amenities as movies, a hospitality hour, and an onboard guide.

THE CALIFORNIA *Zephyr*

The entire length of the Zephyr's journey offers a tremendous diversity of scenery, but a truly spectacular section of magnificent landscape lines the Zephyr's route through the Rocky Mountains. In fact, the California Zephyr follows the same tracks as the AOE between Denver and Salt Lake City. If you are only interested in that portion of the journey, you can take the Zephyr between Denver and Salt Lake City in either direction, traveling mostly in daylight. The Zephyr leaves Denver daily at 9:20 A.M., arriving in Salt Lake City at 12:01 A.M. The eastbound train leaves Salt Lake City at 4:35 A.M., arriving in Denver at 7:40 P.M. In both cases, you travel through the Rockies in daylight, except on the shortest days of winter.

If you find yourself in Denver or Salt Lake City for an extra day or even if you plan this shorter route as a specific travel itinerary, you won't be disappointed. The beauty of the Rockies and the history of the California Zephyr make this a very special train trip.

The *American Orient Express* begins its journey in Denver. A welcome reception and orientation is typically offered in the evening, when passengers board the train. Dinner is served in the train's dining car, and then excited travelers spend their first night on board at the Denver station. The next morning the train departs, allowing a full day to view the spectacular scenery through the twisting canyons, cascading waters, and intriguing rock formations of the Colorado Rocky Mountains.

You may be anxious for the momentum of the trip to begin, but, if your travel arrangements permit, you might want to spend a day or two sight-seeing in Denver before the train departs. An interesting mix of the "Old West" and a modern city, Denver was founded in 1858 when the discovery of gold flakes in the waters of Cherry Creek and the South Platte River unleashed the great "Pike's Peak or Bust" gold rush. The city has continued to boom thanks to oil, mining, and high-tech industries, and it is one of the nation's fastest growing metropolitan areas.

It is no exaggeration that Denver is the "mile-high city." On the steps of the State Capitol, you can stand *exactly* 5,280 feet above sea level. If you're coming from sea level, you'll likely feel some physical effects of the

The elegant interior of the AOE's *vintage cars enhances the romance of the trip.*

The jagged peaks, rushing rivers, and big-sky panoramas of the northern Rockies create one of America's greatest scenic wonders.

altitude in Denver and even more so in the higher elevations of the days ahead. It is wise to take it easy for the first day or two, drink lots of nonalcoholic liquids, and be sure to use sunscreen at all times when you are outdoors because the sun's rays are more intense here.

While there is a lot to do and see within the city limits, train buffs often migrate to the Colorado Railroad Museum in Golden, about twelve miles west of Denver. The 1880-style depot has 50,000 rare photographs and artifacts, and fifty vintage locomotives and cars are displayed on the grounds. Short steam train rides are offered on weekends, and a model train set steams through a miniature, scaled version of Golden.

If you enjoy having an occasional beer, you might be interested to find that Golden is home to the Coors Brewery, the world's largest single-site brewery. Free tours are available along with informal tastings for anyone

American Orient Express Photo by Carl and Ann Purcell

over twenty-one years old. Denver is at the forefront of the microbrewery trend. In fact, Denver claims that on any given day, as many as thirty beers are on tap here that cannot be purchased anywhere else in the world.

After touring Denver, you'll be drawn into a great sense of anticipation as the *American Orient Express* departs on that first early morning. The Rockies variety show begins as you enjoy breakfast in the dining car and settle into your seat for a dramatic day on the train. With Denver still in sight, the train is already snaking upwards. Mile-high plains begin to buckle and form the foothills on the Front Range, ripples of the great upheaval ahead. "We just retired," says one passenger. "We've been working very hard for thirty-seven years and wanted to get out and see the country. I'm afraid to take a nap because I might miss something."

You, too, may share that sense of expectation. From Denver, the train

follows the route of the historic and highly scenic Denver and Rio Grande Western Railroad. "The high point of the route is coming over the Great Divide, then coming down and seeing these vast canyons and the escarpments and the rocks all around us," says John Borneman. "Whether you're just going along on a regular train ride or going on the *American Orient Express,* you're sitting there with these wide windows and you have a panoramic view on either side." Borneman is one of the lecturers that the *AOE* takes on the trip to provide passengers with insights and information about the journey. An expert on birds of the west and on western history, John is also an enthusiastic rail traveler. "Trains are kind of welded into our landscape, and they become a part of that landscape," he says. "There's no such thing as a bad seat on a train." As he speaks, the train grinds its way up long grades and continuous twists and turns. The pace is slow, taking more than seven hours before you reach Grand Junction, 273 rail miles to the west. This is a perfect speed for taking in the almost overwhelming scenic display.

Videotaping the diverse and towering scenery was an especially challenging aspect of producing the PBS documentary of this journey. Positioning themselves between carriages, our two camera operators had to bend and stretch skyward to be able to capture the undulating landscape. Aerial photography taken with a camera mounted on a helicopter also helped bring the wild scenery of this Rocky Mountain trip into the homes of TV viewers.

John Borneman

Amazingly, the terrain becomes even more dramatic as the train gains a mile in elevation in less than an hour and passes through the first of twenty-nine tunnels. Challenged by the increasingly rough landscape, the train crawls up a seemingly endless series of switchback curves, weaving around and through sandstone formations called "hogbacks" and "flatirons." At Rocky, the train negotiates a giant "S" curve to help it gain altitude. On the inside of the upper curve, old rail cars filled with sand are strategically located to protect the train from the high winds that frequently blow through the area, sometimes reaching more than one hundred miles an hour.

Without knowing exactly when it happened, you may suddenly realize that the plains have disappeared and you are in the mountains. To the north, out the right side of the train, is the 14,255-foot Longs Peak; to the south is the 14,264-foot Mount Evans. Below, you can see the 340-foot-high Gross Dam and Reservoir, the primary water supply for Denver. As the train enters the Roosevelt National Forest, you are within sight of the Moffat Tunnel and the towering Continental Divide. If you can narrow your focus away from the larger panorama, you can sometimes spot deer and elk on the slopes above the track.

While enjoyed mostly by tourists today, this train route was originally built out of economic necessity. Established train routes through Wyoming to the north and New Mexico to the south threatened to completely bypass Colorado, with the resulting loss of commerce. An existing rail line going west from Denver proved ineffective because of the nearly impossible route over Rollins Pass. Even in the best conditions, trains needed five hours to cross the Continental Divide around the 13,260-foot James Peak, and winter storms sometimes caused delays of days and weeks. The answer was a tunnel through the mountain, and in 1928 the 6.2-mile Moffat Tunnel was opened, reducing the journey to a mere nine minutes.

The trip through Moffat Tunnel is a great treat for train travelers. You sit in near total darkness as the train passes beneath the Continental Divide. Only occasional red emergency lights break the darkness. Coming out of the tunnel, blinking from the sudden bright light, you are all at once in a different environment, with different weather and different trees and rock formations from those on the eastern side of the tunnel. Three interconnecting mountains are responsible for a tremendous variety of terrain in this densely wooded region famous for its pine trees. The skies are often clear and blue, with a crispness in the air during fall and spring, but the area can be covered by dense fog, almost as if a cloud has stopped for a rest. That is precisely what happens during snow season, when clouds stalled by the mountain range turn the slopes into a snowy playground. We soon pass the town of Winter Park, a popular ski destination for Denver resi-

The train follows the Colorado River into Byers Canyon

BUILDING THE MOFFAT TUNNEL

In 1866 the Union Pacific Railroad bypassed Denver in building the transcontinental railroad when it was decided that a new line from Denver over Rollins Pass would be impossible to build and maintain. Instead, the Union Pacific was built along easier grades through southern Wyoming.

Colorado was convinced that unless a rail link could be kept open to the west,

Two and a half million pounds of dynamite and one thousand workmen were needed to complete Moffat Tunnel. Twenty-eight men lost their lives during construction.

the flow of commerce would bypass the state. The problem was Rollins Pass. "[The previously existing rail line] was twenty-nine miles over the pass," says Don Hulse. "In the summertime, it was beautiful. But for six months a year, or seven sometimes, it was very miserable up there." An Amtrak conductor who comes from a long line of Colorado railroaders, Don Hulse knows every foot of this route, including Rollins Pass. "The snow drifts on Rollins Pass were up to thirty feet at times. Sometimes [railroad workers] were up there a month at a time in the wintertime trying to get the railroad opened because of the snow, snow slides, and avalanches. They just had a real dickens of a time trying to keep the railroad open in the wintertime."

Three times, the state turned down requests to fund a tunnel. The rail line over the Continental Divide was deemed so important, however, that in the spring of 1922 the state finally provided $6.72 million to build one. "The Moffat Tunnel took four years to build, from 1923 to 1927," says Hulse. "They drilled both from the east side and the west side. On the east side, they had to drill and blast through solid rock, and the west side had to shore up and dig out." Two and a half million pounds of dynamite and one thousand workmen were needed before it was done. Twenty-eight men lost their lives. In the end the tunnel cost more than $23 million to complete. It was such an important accomplishment that President Calvin Coolidge pushed a button from the White House triggering the holing-through blast.

In stark contrast to the danger of building it, passenger trains have been safely emerging from Moffat Tunnel every day since its opening more than seventy years ago. "Moffat Tunnel got the

The Moffatt Tunnel cost more than $23 million to build, nearly four times the original estimate.

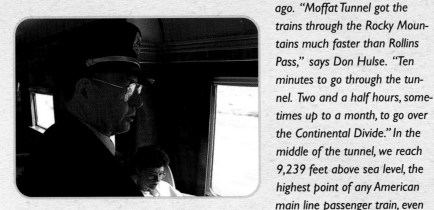

trains through the Rocky Mountains much faster than Rollins Pass," says Don Hulse. "Ten minutes to go through the tunnel. Two and a half hours, sometimes up to a month, to go over the Continental Divide." In the middle of the tunnel, we reach 9,239 feet above sea level, the highest point of any American main line passenger train, even

Don Hulse

though we're still a half-mile underground.

As you approach Moffat Tunnel today, you can still see the remnants of the original route over Rollins Pass. Look to the right just before entering the tunnel westbound.

AMERICAN ORIENT EXPRESS PHOTO BY CARL AND ANN PURCELL

dents and the center of activity in this area.

On this side of the Divide, the streams flow westward, in the opposite direction from those on the eastern side. The sparkling beauty of the trout-filled Fraser River, where President Eisenhower often came to fish, parallels the path of the train through Arapaho National Forest. Later, the Fraser joins the mighty Colorado River, which the train follows for the next 238 miles of the trip. This is the longest stretch in which a river and a railroad share paths in America and one of the longest stretches of a river followed by a railroad in the world.

Even though it is only the sixth longest river in North America, the Colorado seems to outshine all competitors in creating natural wonders. This is, after all, the river that dug the Grand Canyon. From its origin in the Rocky Mountains of Colorado, the river flows southwest 1,470 miles into the Gulf of California in Mexico. Along the way, it descends 10,000 feet before reaching the Pacific Ocean. As a result, it's more like a waterfall than a river in some stretches, useless for transportation but full of thrills for rafters. The canyons and rapids of the upper basin are practically impassable.

The Colorado River ushers the train into a series of canyons, each of which seems determined to outdo the others in spectacle and originality. This is where the breathtaking, unparalleled scenery of this trip really begins. Nothing a human can build can match these marvels provided by Nature.

Byers Canyon is a short, jagged chasm that forces the train to screech around the sharpest mainline rail curve in the country. Rocky cliffs tower high above the train as necks crane to capture the views. Motorists on Highway 40, on the other side of the river, slip through the canyon in five or six minutes. The *American Orient Express* is in no such hurry. "I remember driving [that route] one time years ago and how agonizing it was to try and drive and see the scenery," recalls a passenger. "This way, you're in the captain's seat, and you get to sit back and relax and absorb it all." In some places the canyon walls rise almost straight over the tracks. The railroad has strung cables overhead to protect the tracks from falling rock, a precaution that adds to the sense of adventure.

Many passengers enjoy the passage of the afternoon just relaxing and soaking up the scenery, but there's actually a lot going on up and down the train. "How's everything going for you folks?" asks Scott Gaghan, the train's hotel manager on this trip. Scott is in charge of making sure everything runs smoothly on the *American Orient Express* and that each passenger has a rewarding experience. "The train is almost a quarter-mile long, and to supervise what's happening over a quarter-mile span takes good planning, time management, and also walking back and forth throughout the train, checking with different employees," he says. Hardly skipping a beat, he adds that it also helps to have the foresight to predict the movement of the train while pouring a glass of wine and handling all the glassware and other fragile items that are required to run a hotel moving at eighty miles per hour down the track. Scott has worked on many cruise ships and finds the train journey an interesting alternative for travelers. "I see the *American Orient Express* as bringing

Scott Gaghan

The tracks follow the Colorado River for most of the first day of the trip. Parts of the mighty Colorado are considered unnavigable except for adventurous kayakers and rafters.

The New York Observation Car

Passing through Gore Canyon

back a piece of the past," he says, "an opportunity to experience and relive those memories that a lot of folks—your grandparents, your parents—had as a child."

During the course of the day, you enjoy a comfortable lunch on board the train. By late afternoon, you're ready for a little pick-me-up, so the *AOE* staff serves afternoon tea and cookies in the club cars, just one more special touch that is part of the *American Orient Express* experience.

Just as you enjoy the relaxing pace, so does the Colorado River. The momentarily placid Colorado lures us gently into Gore Canyon, a stretch so rugged that construction engineers who planned the railroad thought seriously about abandoning the canyon and routing the tracks up over the mountain ridge. In the end, they decided to continue clinging to the river's banks. With sheer rock walls of 1,500 feet, it is easy to see why Gore Canyon is accessible only by train. "You look up and you see cliffs a thousand feet up. If you look down, you see some of the rocks that have come down and are in the river and they, of course, cause the rapids," observes veteran Amtrak train conductor Don Hulse. "They don't allow rafting in Gore Canyon unless you have a special permit and you can see why. There are rocks in the water that are really treacherous. Looks like fun, but it's very treacherous."

The excitement created by the awesome nature of the canyon has no time to subside. Soon the *AOE* reaches another canyon so deep and forbidding that it was thought impassable by some. Glenwood Canyon's brightly colored rocks, cliffs, aspen trees, and evergreens proliferate as the train follows the river through the canyon. Many early trappers and Native Americans chose to climb over the mesa and circle the canyon to continue their journey. Railroad engineers were the first to cut a permanent passageway along the base of the canyon. Today it's also the path of Interstate 70, the most recently completed segment of America's interstate highway sys-

tem and one of the most elaborate and challenging to construct. Built at a cost of $500 million, I–70 was completed in 1992. Much of its expense can be attributed to the efforts made to preserve the natural landscape as much as possible.

For half an hour the train twists through this beautiful gorge. It's easy to allow your imagination to roam. "When we went through that gully, those enormous, craggy rocks rose right up beside us on both sides and they look like castles," notes a passenger. "And I kept thinking one of the princesses should be peeking her head out and looking down at us. It was so beautiful and so very, very high. With the river flowing along beside us and the rocks going up, it's just breathtaking, really."

The train passes through Feather River Canyon, one of several canyons that can only be seen from the train —or by an extremely adventurous hiker.

The Vista-Dome cars of the famous California Zephyr were inspired by the views in Glenwood Canyon.

Indeed, the remarkable beauty of Glenwood Canyon inspired a new kind of railroad passenger car back in the 1940s. Called the Vista-Dome, it was a car with a glass canopy, tailor-made for travel in the Rocky Mountains where the scenery is not just around you but overhead. In 1944 a rail executive was riding through Glenwood Canyon in the cab of a Rio Grande locomotive. "And he got thinkin'," says conductor Don Hulse, "'why can't people see what I can see from this engine.' He got to Salt Lake City that night and spent most of the night in his hotel room drawing pictures of passenger cars and eventually came up with the bubble top, and it was known as the Vista-Dome car." Beginning in 1949, the glass-topped Vista-Domes became a feature of the *California Zephyr* passenger trains, traveling from Oakland to Chicago. The Vista-Domes were retired in 1970.

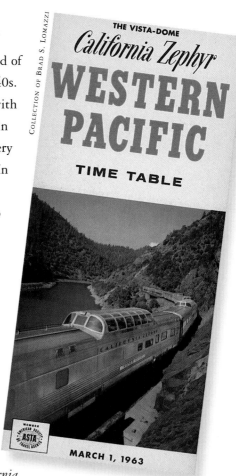

THE VISTA-DOME
California Zephyr
WESTERN PACIFIC
TIME TABLE

MARCH 1, 1963

As the train emerges from Glenwood Canyon, it cruises through the center of Glenwood Springs. The *AOE* doesn't stop here, but this is a busy stop for Amtrak's *California Zephyr* bringing skiers in winter to nearby Aspen. Glenwood Springs is the home of one of the world's largest outdoor hot-water swimming pools. You can see the 600-foot-long pool out the right side of the train across the river. Built by a British investment company in 1891, it was the main attraction of a resort created here at the same time. Among its many patrons was infamous gunslinger Doc Holiday, who came to Glenwood Springs to restore his health. Also a card wizard, Holiday was one of the participants in the gunfight at the O.K. Corral in Tombstone, Arizona, in 1881. He died

Glenwood Canyon

in Glenwood Springs in 1887 and is buried in the town cemetery.

Departing Glenwood Springs, the train winds its way through the Colorado River Valley, which is encased by the red stratified mountains that typify this region of the Rockies. Watch for rafters on the Roaring Fork River, which joins the Colorado on the left. Soon you pass through Debeque Canyon, which looks like the setting for an old western movie. As the train emerges from the canyon, the landscape changes. You have entered the famed fruit growing region of Colorado's Western Slope, an area that produces large quantities of peaches and apricots. Fruit orchards define the approach to Grand Junction, western Colorado's largest city. The broken cliffs of the Colorado National Monument border the route on the left. Once heavily populated by dinosaurs, this region has important skeletal remains.

After passing the town of Mack, the train emerges from a short tunnel and follows the Colorado River into the spectacular Ruby Canyon. This twenty-mile stretch is very wild and scenic. The train winds through brightly colored rocks carved by the Colorado River out of the

Passengers enjoy dinner and sleep onboard the AOE as it makes its way to Salt Lake City, the first off-train excursion.

AMERICAN ORIENT EXPRESS PHOTO BY CARL AND ANN PURCELL

Uncompahgre Plateau, and bald and golden eagles can often be seen riding the currents of air along the canyon walls and across the river below.

As the train crosses the border from Colorado to Utah, you lose sight of the magnificent Colorado River as it heads southwest toward its master-piece, the Grand Canyon in Arizona. With the departure of the Colorado River, canyonlands are quickly replaced by a vast expanse of desert terrain. Over the next 150 miles, the stark mesa tops of the Roan Cliffs stand stoically as the train weaves through cuts and

Red Canyon

gullies across the barren landscape. Deprived of water, the land begins to resemble the surface of Mars. These eerie forms, lit by the setting sun, signal the end of your first day of sight-seeing from the train.

As passengers relax and enjoy dinner and refreshments, the train's staff converts the sitting rooms into sleepers. The light fades on the desert scene as you roll through the night on a gradual swing north. It has been an incredible day, unquestionably one of the best single-day train journeys in North America. In the morning, you arrive at your first off-board stop—Salt Lake City, Utah's capital and largest city.

The *American Orient Express* allows a full day to explore Salt Lake City. On the western edge of the Rockies, Salt Lake City is best known as the headquarters of the Church of Jesus Christ of Latter Day Saints. Although

Dan Rascon

Jim Bricker first discovered the Great Salt Lake in 1824, it wasn't until 1847 that a group of Mormons, led by Brigham Young, arrived at the current site of Salt Lake City and decided to settle there. When they leave the train, most travelers head downtown to Temple Square, Utah's number-one tourist attraction. "It's a beautiful place to us because it's of great significance," says church spokesman Dan Rascon. "It's a place where Brigham Young came and built back 150 years ago. It's a place where many people come from all over the world to visit, learn about the church, and be able to experience a little bit about what we believe in."

Many travelers consider a visit to the famed Tabernacle to
be the highlight of the tour. "The tabernacle is one that everyone is always excited to come in and take a look at because of
the Mormon Tabernacle Choir," says Rascon. "It was a building
that Brigham Young felt needed to be built in order to accom-
modate large congregations of people. When you walk in, it is a
feeling of awe because of the size of it, because of the way it's
structured, because of the designs and everything about it."

Inside the Tabernacle

Small groups tour the building and are treated to a demonstration of its
legendary acoustics. A small pin is dropped on stage, and you can hear it
from 150 feet away at the back of the hall.

You probably won't have any trouble guessing the number-two attraction of Salt Lake City. The Great Salt Lake is one of America's most famous
and unusual natural phenomena, with 2,100 square miles of water—but

don't try to drink it. Only the Dead
Sea is saltier than this lake, which is
eight times saltier than the ocean.
"The Great Salt Lake is often erro-
neously referred to as a 'dead sea',"
says Tim Smith, a ranger at Antelope
Island State Park. It may not have a
large number of species—it's really

Ranger Tim Smith

only algae, brine shrimp, and brine flies—but these three are present in
incredible numbers. Several kinds of wildlife exist on the island, including its
namesake, the Pronghorn Antelope—and, seemingly out of place, a herd of
bison. By the late 1800s civilization had driven these animals to
the brink of extinction. But in 1893 some Utah conservationists
brought twelve buffaloes to Antelope Island, hoping the surrounding lake would insulate them from danger and allow them
to grow. Those twelve bison are now a herd of more than 600.

Several rivers feed into Great Salt Lake, but it retains such a
high level of salt because no streams empty from the lake. Salt
and other minerals carried by the streams simply stay in the lake.
Like the lake that surrounds it, Antelope Island seems desolate at first, but
you can easily fill a day sightseeing here. "Antelope Island is the best place to

*The Tabernacle was completed in
1893.*

A passenger spots an erupting geyser.

Part of the excitement of riding the train is the unexpected, says lecturer John Borneman. "You get all these different views and sensations that you can't get any other way."

experience the Great Salt Lake," says ranger Smith. "You're in the middle of the lake, and the views are stunning. It is a distance away from the city, but within sight of it—and so you have wildness with a backdrop of the largest metropolitan area in the state."

After a day exploring Salt Lake City, the *AOE* is on the move again, weaving north and west along the foothills of the Wasatch Range. As the train parallels the western rim of the Rockies, several hours of daylight are still available to allow you to enjoy the scenery of northern Utah. Along the route, Bear River Canyon furnishes one of the most impressive canyon rail trips in the West. Only three miles long, it is nonetheless thrilling as the train passes along the eastern edge of the cliffs, through short tunnels,

over trestles, and around abrupt juts of rock. The nearby Bear River Migratory Bird Refuge is home to seasonal populations of ducks, geese, and shorebirds. Twilight is a particularly good time to watch for these birds. Below the train, the Bear River rushes by. As nightfall approaches, passengers enjoy another wonderful meal in the ambience of this rolling gourmet restaurant. The night is spent on the train heading through Idaho.

Although you've already seen some spectacular mountain scenery from the unique vantage point of the train, you spend the next two days getting an even closer look at the Rockies. The *AOE* itinerary allows for a full day each at Yellowstone National Park and Grand Teton National Park. You need to travel a few hours by bus to get to each of the parks from where the train is parked, and the time on the bus is the biggest downside of the trips. Still, getting to see some of the highlights of these two spectacular parks is a great addition to this train journey. Then, if you really want to explore these destinations further, you can plan to come back when you have more time to linger.

The railroad has always been important to these two national parks. "The train played an exceptionally large role in early Yellowstone," says park archivist Lee Whittlesey. "Beginning in 1883, the Northern Pacific Railroad came to the north entrance. So virtually all early visitors came by train, got on a stagecoach, and took five to ten days to go around the park."

NATIONAL PARK SERVICE

During high water in June, more than 64,000 gallons of water per second tumble over Yellowstone's Lower Falls.

In contrast, most visits these days are more likely to resemble your one-day dash through the park.

Yellowstone is the world's first national park, and every trip here requires a stop at the park's best-known landmark. "Old Faithful is the world's most famous geyser," says park ranger Ann Deutch. "It's big, averaging 140 feet tall. It's frequent, usually twenty times a day, and the power of Old Faithful is astonishing." Deutch has seen Old Faithful more than 10,000 times, but she never tires of it. "No two eruptions are the same, just like snowflakes," she says.

Hundreds of bison make their home at Yellowstone.

Rudyard Kipling called Yellowstone "3,000 square miles of freaks of fiery nature." When you visit Yellowstone's Fountain Paint Pot, you get to see many fiery freaks at once. The seemingly refreshing blue water is actually scalding hot from subterranean fires. The bones of an animal are visible through the clear water—most likely a buffalo that got too close trying to keep warm in winter. You see fumaroles and mud pots, cauldrons of volcanic burps turning rock into clay mud. "Hell bubbling up," one old trapper surmised. More than 10,000 hot springs are in Yellowstone, more than in all the rest of the world combined. "Here," says Ann Deutch, "we tolerate the fact that nature is more powerful than we are. It's a wonderful lesson."

Beautiful Jenny Lake in Grand Teton National Park

For two parks so close together, Yellowstone and Grand Teton are very different. "Yellowstone is a vast upland plateau with incredible geothermal features that you'll not find anywhere else in the world," says Grand Teton park ranger Linda Olson. "What it's not is the vertical magnificence of a big mountain range and that's what you get when you drive twenty miles down the road from Yellowstone to Grand Teton." Linda has been a park ranger at Grand Teton for nearly thirty years. "Grand Teton has been referred to as a windshield park because people drive the roads of the park with their eyes plastered on the mountains. It's just a view you can't take your eyes off."

Although there's a lot to enjoy at Grand Teton National Park, it has one site that seems to draw every visitor. "Probably the most spectacular place, and the place that every visitor goes, is Jenny Lake," says Linda Olson. "Jenny is a spectacular oval, a brilliant blue sapphire that sits at the heart of the Tetons. Jenny is one of the string of valley lakes that lie at the end of a canyon where the glaciers came down, scoured out a big hole, and when they melted filled the hole with water. Now it's fed by snow melt and mountain streams." Linda Olson has made her home in the mountain area since 1972. It's a place she clearly loves and enjoys sharing with others. "These are America's Alps," she says. "These are friendly mountains and what they do is they become a part of you." About half the visitors to Grand Teton National Park are repeat visitors. "It calls them back," Linda says. "You can't resist returning to the mountains."

Linda Olson

Just outside Grand Teton National Park is the town of Jackson, Wyoming. Once a fur-trading center, Jackson has turned itself into a boomtown catering to skiers and tourists year-round. You have a few hours to stroll Jackson's boardwalk and its many shops, which are a nice respite from the wilderness activities and provide a brief fix to those who include shopping as a major part of any trip. "Jackson is our major gateway city for this park," says Grand Teton's Linda Olson. "It's Western. It has great big antler arches on the corner of the town square. It retains a Western flavor and yet it's got big-town stuff."

The antler arch in Jackson, Wyoming

After two days exploring some of the most remarkable mountain scenery in the United States, you reboard the *American Orient Express* for the final leg of the journey. The last night onboard includes a grand farewell dinner and is filled with excited conversations with fellow passengers about the week's events. Conductor Don Hulse, who has made this trip hundreds of times, best sums up the experience: "I never get bored going through the Rockies," he says. "There's always something of beauty to see."

THE TRAIN:

The Skeena *is one of Via Rail's premier passenger trains serving northwest Canada. It offers coach and first-class accommodations, plus onboard food and beverage service. There are no sleeping accommodations available on board.*

THE ROUTE:

The Skeena *travels through some of the most spectacular wilderness scenery available from a train in North America as it goes from the town of Jasper in Alberta Province through the Rocky Mountains of British Columbia to the port of Prince Rupert on the Pacific Ocean.*

DURATION OF THE TRIP:

The Via Rail trip takes two days to travel the 720 miles between Jasper and Prince Rupert with one scheduled overnight stop in Prince George. You are on the train for about twenty hours during the two days.

HIGHLIGHTS:

The close proximity of the passing train to the wilderness scenery is the highlight of this journey. Passengers can add stops at any of the small, quaint towns that dot the route, most of which offer a tremendous diversity of outdoor activities, including fishing, hiking, boating, and sight-seeing. Wildlife and ancient native cultures add to the sense of discovery on this trip.

As if deliberately designed to appeal to the adventurer, Via Rail's Skeena *train travels through some of the most remote and beautiful country that can be seen from a train anywhere in Canada.*

THE CANADIAN
R O C

DURING ITS TWO-DAY JOURNEY, THE SKEENA crosses 191 bridges and travels through fourteen tunnels, passing snow-capped mountain peaks, glaciers, waterfalls, raging rivers, rich green forests, pristine lakes, and Native American villages with famed totem poles. From the parapets of the Canadian Rocky Mountains to the wild and scenic Pacific Coast, this journey is a unique way to explore the sparsely populated and ruggedly scenic area of Canada's British Columbia province.

Drawn by the unknown and by the call of its vastness, visitors from all over the world are attracted to the *Skeena*. "A lot of our guests are Americans and Europeans," says Via Rail's Anita Marple. "They find the distance just so incredible—the concept of going for hundreds of miles with no communities or no people. That in itself is quite amazing." Anita has worked on the rails in Canada for nearly twenty years, first as a conductor and now as an engineer. "You can come along here and see hundreds of waterfalls, and then the valley opens wider and wider and you come to the ocean. They're mostly just thrilled," she says of *Skeena's* passengers. "They think they've had the trip of a lifetime, and they have."

KIES

The *Skeena* runs for more than 700 miles through the mostly inaccessible and largely undeveloped scenic wilderness of British Columbia, and just about everything this train journey has to offer is found right along the tracks. The ever-changing scenery is just outside the big windows of the Via Rail passenger coaches, and British Columbia's history is close to the surface along the *Skeena*'s route. The ancient traditions of the native peoples, the not-so-distant pioneer days of gold panning, and the more familiar forms of modern history all have left their marks at the side of the tracks.

In fact, dozens of small towns and villages in this otherwise isolated wilderness owe their very existence to the train. Many of the towns along the route are so small that, for the brief moments when the train passes, their populations are doubled or even quadrupled. "When the railway was being constructed, about every three to five miles of railway track they would have some kind of community," says Bruce Wilkenson, who came to British Columbia in 1979 on a family vacation and stayed, operating a river guide business for tourists. "You'd be amazed at what you can find all the way through to the coast, as far as buildings and towns," he says. "Many just are no more, and they were such small places that there isn't a real big written history about them." While many of these places no longer exist or survive only as a few old buildings or an abandoned train station, some of the towns have grown beyond their initial dependency on the railroad. The *Skeena*'s route is punctuated with communities that came into existence because of the railroad but now offer many

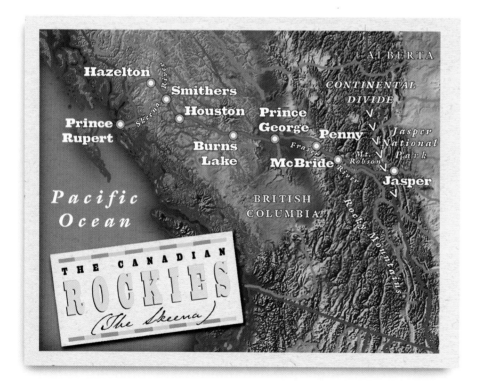

surprises and treats to the unhurried traveler. "All of the communities along here are very tourist oriented," says Anita Marple. "They want people to come and to see some of the most beautiful country in the world."

Once an overnight train, the *Skeena* used to make the trip from Jasper to Prince Rupert in twenty-one straight hours. Luckily for its riders, the railroad wisely decided that the trip was too beautiful to spend half of it in darkness. Now the *Skeena* stops overnight at Prince George. If you just want to enjoy the scenery and the ambience of the train, the *Skeena*'s regular two-day itinerary is fine, but most people spend a few days in the communities at the beginning, along the way, or at the end of the route. Without much effort you can put together an itinerary that allows you to explore the astonishing wilderness territory, tour the picturesque towns, learn about the region's native cultures, and enjoy just about any outdoor recreational activity. The train makes about a half-dozen scheduled stops and offers about two dozen "flag stops" where the *Skeena* can drop you off and pick you up on request. Each community along this route has a distinctive character and a variety of attractions. Whether you are already a passionate outdoor enthusiast or a mere dabbler in adventure, you can indulge in wilderness activities such as hiking, rafting, fishing, wildlife observation, or heli-hiking. You might also try just plain relaxing amidst the great beauty of the Canadian Rockies.

Giant Mount Robson looms over the westbound Skeena *train. On clear days, passengers on the* Skeena *have several opportunities to see the mountain.*

HELI-HIKING

The Rocky Mountains of northern Canada are a labyrinth of peaks, valleys, and glaciers, inaccessible to all but the most skilled mountaineers. Fortunately for less adventurous travelers, the Skeena cuts through some of this remote mountain wilderness and provides a unique way to view the scenery. While there are myriad opportunities to explore the wilderness at closer range, it is nevertheless difficult for the casual traveler to get a true "wild" experience. After all, getting into the wilderness typically takes more time and effort than most of us are willing, or able, to give.

Increasingly, helicopters provide a way for tourists to explore the mountain wilderness of the Canadian Rockies. So-called heli-hiking has become increasingly popular, and helicopter tours offer a range of options. Some sightseers choose to enjoy the scenery from the air and experience the thrill of a helicopter ride. Others are "taxied" into the backcountry to hike alone or with a guide in otherwise inaccessible wilderness. Some lodges and resorts offer multi-day packages that include a day of heli-hiking.

For the production of the television program on the Skeena rail journey, our crew joined a group of tourists for a day of heli-hiking with a local tour company, Canadian Mountain Holidays. "This is God's country," says guide Werner Numsen. "With the helicopter, we can bring people here who have never experienced anything like this." Numsen is an experienced mountain climber, a necessary companion when traveling to remote glaciers and mountaintops. "You need a guide who will explain things to make it safe and enjoyable," he says. Hiking parties are grouped by

Heli-hikers crossing the glacier

Werner Numsen

their preferred level of difficulty, and safety is a prime concern. "I like to go single file because there are a lot of crevasses," Numsen tells his attentive novices. "Just remember to walk where I walk," he cautions, "and when you don't see me, don't follow."

Heli-hikers are ferried to several different locations on a typical day trip so that they can enjoy a range of mountain wilderness experiences. "Right now, we're on the North Canoe Glacier," Numsen tells his group of heli-hikers. "This would be a very difficult place to come without a helicopter." Later, the heli-hikers are transported to a point high above the glacier they just crossed. "You can see where we hiked on the glacier," Numsen tells the tired but exhilarated tourists. As they stand on what feels like the edge of the world, everyday life seems very distant. "It puts things in perspective for you," says one heli-hiker. "When all you do is work six–seven days a week, you realize there are a lot of things out there that are more important." Even for an experienced climber like Werner Numsen, the mountain never loses its magic or mystery. "This for me is a very spiritual place. If you don't like it, I can't help you."

The starting point for the westbound *Skeena* train is Jasper. Like so many communities along this route, Jasper is here because the rails are here. A mountain getaway now, Jasper's past is intricately intertwined with

the quest by Canadians to link their country's coasts and open up a trade route to the Orient. Harry Holm, or "the Railroad Guy" as he is known in Jasper, knows the history of this route about as well as anyone. Harry's father was a railroad man, and Harry, who is now

Jasper's "Railroad Guy"
Harry Holm

retired, started working on the railroad when he was sixteen. "In 1911 the steel arrived in Jasper. They had to send ships and men and materials all the way around South America and up the coast," Harry says. "They started up against incredible odds. They couldn't even see where they were going. The bush was so dense you had to climb a tree to see where you were."

Today Jasper is a bustling tourist town of shops, eateries, and nightspots with plenty of outdoor activities in its immediate surroundings. About 4,000 people live in Jasper, but each summer the population swells with vacationers as thousands of people from all over the world come here to get away from each other. The summer months can be quite crowded in Jasper, so it's always wise to book reservations ahead of time. The lure of the majestic mountains is what draws the people here—the town lies at the northern end of Jasper National Park, Canada's largest mountain national park. You won't find much in the way of lodging near the park, but most of the park's major attractions are easily reachable as day trips from town.

One of Jasper National Park's most impressive attractions is Athabasco Falls, forged as the Athabasco River squeezes through a narrow gorge. Easy-to-reach overlooks and an interpretative trail provide great views and photo opportunities. Indisputably, this is a land of superlatives. Mount Edith Cavell, at 11,033 feet, is the highest mountain near Jasper, and Maligne Lake is one of the largest glacier-fed lakes in the world. The beauty of the lake led to the creation of the park and to its popularity with visitors. Very crowded with cars in the peak summer months, this area offers several excellent walking trails around the lake. Being on the water itself,

Elk in the town of Jasper,
Alberta Province

After crossing the Continental Divide, the Skeena *hugs the shoreline of Moose Lake, one of the largest lakes along this stretch of the route.*

however, is the best way to appreciate the beauty of the place. Tour cruises are offered, or you can rent a boat and go out on your own.

Though it's hard to upstage the scenery, other forms of natural beauty also abound here. Many people come to Jasper—the town and the park—to view the wildlife, and normally you don't have to go far to see animals at very close range. It is not unusual to see elk and mule deer casually stroll down Main Street of Jasper. On many days an elk herd makes itself at home on the streets of Jasper, casually nibbling grass and gazing curiously back at the tourists.

Via Rail's Jasper Station

After exploring Jasper, you board the *Skeena* for an early afternoon departure. The *Skeena* is easily recognizable by its gleaming stainless steel cars. Put in service in 1955, these cars are popular with rail fans because they retain the feel of 1950s luxury train travel. Completely restored, they offer an elegant style that has been enhanced by graceful etched glass and original Canadian artwork. During the peak tourist season between May and

October, the *Skeena* usually has three passenger cars. One is for coach passengers, and two serve first-class passengers (what Via Rail calls its Totem Class, named for the many totem poles found along this route). The Park Car is one of the Totem Class coaches and includes a dome section that seats twenty-four passengers and provides terrific views. The Park Car also has two lounges that seat about twenty passengers. Food and beverage service is available throughout the trip, and each trip has a service manager whose job is to provide onboard services and information for passengers.

The Skeena's *dome car provides excellent views.*

The *Skeena,* like many Via Rail trains, is smaller than its passenger counterparts in the United States, allowing for lots of time to get to know your fellow passengers as you relax and enjoy the scenery. "For some reason, trains bring out the socialite in people," says Via Rail locomotive engineer John Howarth. "People that normally don't really talk, when

they're a captive audience on a train they talk. And a lot of people that take the train will tell you they do it for that reason, that they've made some of the best friends they've ever had on the train." John is a second-generation Canadian railroader and the engineer on part of the *Skeena* trip. "People meet their mates for life on the train," John says. "There's just some magic about taking the train. If you want to get somewhere quick, take the bus, but if you want to have a good time while you're getting there, take the trains."

The first day's journey takes a little over six hours and covers about one-third of the distance to the sea. This leg of the trip is full of great scenery but offers few opportunities for off-train excursions. The train route parallels the path of four different mountain rivers, following water nearly the entire length of the trip. The stunning scenery begins almost immediately as the train leaves Jasper and slowly climbs along the Miette River, hugging the rugged rock face of the Victoria Cross Range. Wire fences along the uphill side of the tracks are rockslide detectors that activate a warning signal for train engineers in case of a rockslide or avalanche. As passengers settle into their comfortable seats, the conversation and mood drift far from everyday life. The train serves as a kind of space capsule, providing a close encounter with the wilderness of the surrounding land. This early part of the route is a good time to look for hawks soaring above the tracks and moose and elk at the edge of the woods or along streams.

Soon afterward, the *Skeena* crosses the border from Alberta into British Columbia and crests the Continental Divide at Yellowhead Pass. At only 3,718 feet, Yellowhead Pass is one of the lowest points along the entire North American Continental Divide, and its surrounding mountain peaks, which reach more than 11,000 feet, dwarf the train. Yellowhead Lake stretches out from the tracks, and you can see Mount Fitzwilliam and Mount Rockingham across the lake.

Before long, one of the scenic highlights of the journey comes into view. At 12,972 feet, Mount Robson is the highest peak in the Canadian Rockies. Often referred to as "the Dome," its sheer rock sides and crown of snow are an unforgettable sight. Mount Robson Provincial Park was estab-

Mount Robson is one of British Columbia's most impressive sights and a highlight of the Skeena *trip. At 12,973 feet it is the highest peak in the Canadian Rockies.*

lished in 1913 to preserve the peak and surrounding area. The 838-square-mile park is populated by snow-covered mountain peaks, endless forests, deep canyons, and icy, rushing rivers. You can catch glimpses of Mount Robson for several miles, although clouds often obscure its peak. This postcard panorama of Mount Robson from the train provides a humbling start to this rail journey.

Before the mountain passes from sight, the *Skeena* joins up with the Fraser River and follows it all the way to Prince George. From its source in

Bruce Wilkenson leads a float trip down the Fraser River.

Yellowhead Lake, the clear waters of the Fraser River flow 850 miles to the Strait of Georgia at Vancouver, providing the powerful and regal chinook salmon with one of the longest spawning migrations in North America. "That big dark shadow up ahead of us is another salmon," says river guide Bruce Wilkenson, whose company, Mount Robson Adventures, offers float trips to tourists. Our camera crew accompanied Bruce as he paddled a group of tourists down the river in a big yellow raft. "We're gonna get out here to have a look at some salmon. If you come here, you can see the salmon right here in front of us," Bruce

MATTHEW G. WHEELER

says. "There are five species of salmon in the Pacific Ocean. The chinook is the biggest, coho, sockeye, chums and pinks." Bruce's float trips are a great way to discover the Fraser River, learn a little about salmon, and enjoy an incredibly relaxing few hours. The formidable Mount Robson looms around nearly every bend of the river. The ribbons of sparkling water run a parallel course with the steel rails along the banks of the Fraser, and the hum of the locomotive can often be heard over the lapping of the river. "The railway runs directly to our right. You can see the two train lines along the mountain," says Bruce Wilkenson. "It was two separate railways built along that ridge. They were built around 1909 to 1914 through this area."

The train follows the Fraser River into the town of McBride, the only scheduled stop on the *Skeena*'s route between Jasper and Prince George. Nestled in the two-mile-wide, 150-mile-long Robson Valley, the farming community of McBride was built in 1912 during the construction of the Grand Trunk Pacific Railroad. Once a railroad boomtown, totally dependent on the trains, it shrunk significantly in population when the track construction crews departed. Today McBride is a town of about 700 residents serving the farming, lumbering, and ranching district of the Robson Valley. Its connection to rail history is evident all over town.

The town of McBride was established during construction of the railroad in 1912. Photographer Matthew Wheeler recalls, "Meeting the train would be an event in itself, and half the town would turn out, but that's all memories now."

After a brief stop to pick up passengers, the *Skeena* continues its jaunt through the scenic Robson Valley. The section between McBride and Prince George is one of the loneliest stretches of the *Skeena*'s route. Only the rhythmic clanking of the rail cars interrupts the quiet of the wilderness. The pace of the train allows time to study the landscape, looking for some remnant of the past. A dozen flag stops are on this portion of the journey, but most are towns of a few hundred people or less. This is prime moose and bear habitat, and it is not unusual for the train to slow down to allow a bear to lazily cross the tracks. The best place to spot a moose is along the river in late afternoon and early evening.

John Howarth

Hemmed in by farmlands and forest, the track follows a winding and meandering course along peaceful stretches of the Fraser River. Locomotive engineer John Howarth runs the *Skeena* between Jasper and Prince George. He's been a railroader for thirty years and has operated locomotives for more than twenty of those. "I grew up in a railroad town. My dad was an engineer," John says. "He worked for CN Rail at the time and he drove steam engines. When I was a little kid I always wanted to do that, and that's what I ended up doing." John stops the train for a ritual straight out of the *Skeena*'s history. The community of Penny is the only remaining "Royal Mail Stop" on Canada's Northern Line. All mail in and out of Penny still goes by rail. Penny is typical of the flag stops along the route. "Basically there's three ways to get into Penny," John Howarth says. "You can come in by rail, you can come in on a crude road, and people that live there use the river to get in and out. But most of the people in Penny still consider themselves to be connected to the outside world by the train."

John frequently spends his days off visiting the friends he's made in Penny and other communities that border the rails.

By early evening, the *Skeena* nears Prince George. The mountains recede into the distance and the interior opens to lakes and

broad plains. After crossing the Fraser River one more time, we enter Prince George, a thriving commercial center of more than 70,000. Known as "the White Spruce Capital of the World," its two main industries are lumbering and mining.

In contrast to the remote, sparsely populated stretches of the first day's trip, Prince George is surprisingly active. A major transportation hub at the crossroads of two highways and two railways, it is where some passengers change trains for other destinations. If you plan to catch the *Skeena* in the morning for the rest of the trip west, Prince George is just a nice place to have dinner and spend the night. You'll find several motels, a few charming B&Bs, and some interesting restaurants to choose from. You might consider spending an extra day or two seeing the sights in and around this area before reboarding the *Skeena* for the trip to Prince Rupert.

Crossing the Fraser River at Prince George

One spot to explore in town is the Fraser Fort George Museum, which offers a good overview of the natural history of Prince George. Here too you find information on the lifestyle and culture of the local Carrier tribe. Intrigued by such topics, you may find it hard to resist the lure of the Great Outdoors. As with many of the stops along the *Skeena*'s route, Prince George is a good place to pursue a wide range of recreational activities, including lake and river fishing. If observation is more your style than participation, you can find lots of places to see wildlife such as bears, mountain goats, moose, and elk in their natural habitat.

Rail fans have an especially good reason to spend some extra time in town. The Prince George Railway and Forest Industry Museum has a notable selection of rail cars, railroad artifacts, and other equipment. The centerpiece of the museum is the *Nechako,* a 1913 Pullman that was beautifully restored for Expo '86, with its polished brass and oak lounge. Outdoors, the Fort George Railway operates a small steam engine that provides rides on a half-mile track. The engine, known as a "dinkey," is similar to those used during the construction of the Grand Trunk Pacific Railway. The station at the Fort George Railway is patterned after a standard design for small stations that was used for more than 200 Grand Trunk Pacific stations in western Canada. Only a few of the original stations remain, including one in Dunster and another in Prince Rupert.

RAILROADS IN CANADA

Railroads have always been important to Canada and its development. The size of the country and its sparse population were major factors in the development of an extensive rail system. By 1900 Canada had more railways per capita than anywhere else in the world. "In other areas, the nation built the railroad," says veteran Canadian railroader Harry Holm, "but in Canada, the railroad built the nation." In many parts of Canada, the train was there first and the people followed later. The train was a way to connect the isolated settlements of the Pacific Coast with the growing cities in the east and, in the process, encourage people to settle in the vast regions in between. Straddling the line between Alberta and British Columbia, the Rocky Mountain range once blocked Canada's western expansion. Canada's first prime minister, Sir John McDonald, had to promise to build a railroad through the mountains as a way of getting the British colonies on the West Coast to agree to join the fledging Confederation.

Canada's first national railroad link was the Canadian Pacific Railway, built from 1881 to 1885. Construction of the railroad was a formidable task, passing through some extremely difficult terrain. The tracks reached from the eastern cities, across the rugged Canadian Shield north of the Great Lakes, through the prairies and mountain passes of the Rockies, and finally to the Pacific coast. The Great Northern Railway (1896–1917) and the Grand Trunk Pacific Railway (1902–1923) laid tracks across the Canadian north to form the second transcontinental link. Later, they joined to become the Canadian National Railway. Both the Canadian Pacific and the Canadian National had extensive freight and passenger networks.

In 1978 the passenger services were combined as Via Rail Canada, the equivalent of Amtrak in the United States. Via Rail provides passenger train service over a 9,000-mile system, extending from coast to coast. It operates 430 trains per week, serving nearly four million passengers annually. The majority of Via Rail's routes run through central Canada, along the border with the United States, where most of Canada's population is concentrated. Trains like the Skeena and the Canadian, however, serve areas that are often inaccessible by other means of transportation.

The Skeena *travels through a vast, remote, and sparsely populated part of North America.*

Early in the morning, the *Skeena* resumes its westward journey. The trip from Prince George to Prince Rupert takes a little over twelve hours and includes seven regular stops and another eight flag stops. If you are interested in exploring more of British Columbia than you can see from the train, you can take advantage of these opportunities to disembark during this leg of the journey.

Leaving Prince George, the *Skeena* follows the Nechako River and moves quickly across the open miles of the great northern plateau. Large ranches, rolling farmland, towering forests of spruce, pine, and fir, and some of the largest natural lakes in British Columbia comprise the diverse landscape. The Carrier Sekani tribe, who first lived in this region centuries ago, traded with the coastal native people and the *Skeena*'s route retraces some of their ancient paths to the coast. The train makes a brief stop at Vanderhoof, a busy center for loggers and ranchers. Every spring and fall, some 50,000 Canada geese find refuge in nearby Nechako Bird Sanctuary, a rest stop on their migration.

The *Skeena* crosses the Endako River eight times before reaching the town of Burns Lake in the heart of the Lakes District. Until the railroad arrived in 1908, Burns Lake was just a telegraph relay cabin. Today it is a major recreational destination, with some of the best trout fishing in British Columbia. It's also an access point to Tweedsmuir Provincial Park, the greatest wilderness park in British Columbia. The area has changed little since it was first explored nearly 200 years ago, and there are still no roads in the park. It is accessible only by boat or floatplane. The Burns Lake area also has an interesting geological history. A huge boulder containing fossils was found in 1986 and is on display at the Lakes District Museum. Just to the south of the Lakes District are the Eagle Creek opal deposits, one of the few places where rare precious stones can be found in western Canada. Rockhounds also search this area for the more common white, amber, and green agates.

Houston, British Columbia, is the next town, and on the way, the *Skeena* crosses the twisting Buckley River eleven times. This region is prime moose country. Soaring bald eagles are also frequently seen in this area, as they are along the rest of the *Skeena*'s route. No surprise: British Columbia is home to one-fourth of the world's bald eagle population.

Scattered between Burns Lake and Price Rupert, like so many sparkling jewels, are hundreds of mountain lakes dug centuries ago by glacial activity. It comes as no shock to learn that this is an area known for the extravagance of its fishing spots. If you are a fishing enthusiast, you may want to work an extra day into your itinerary at Burns Lake or Houston; both are scheduled stops on the *Skeena's* route. One nearby fishing hole earned the name "Millionaire's Pool" because of the celebrities who have fished its waters. Houston (population 3,300) sits where the Morice River joins the Buckley River and is the self-proclaimed "World Steelhead Capital." No one can argue that the Morice is one of the great steelhead fishing rivers in the world. Locals built a sixty-foot-tall aluminum fishing rod as a tribute to the fly-fishing enthusiasts who come to Houston every year.

The *Skeena* pulls into the next regular stop at Smithers around two in the afternoon. A logging town of about 5,000 people, Smithers marks the end of the Interior Plateau. Once a stop on the early fur trade routes, Smithers has a lot to offer if you decide to linger here longer than the ten-minute train stop. Smithers is surrounded by mountain ranges and offers year-round skiing, mountain climbing, rock hunting, and fishing for steelhead or salmon. Established in 1913 as a division point on the Grand Trunk Pacific, it was the first incorporated village in British Columbia. In 1979 many businesses along the town's Main Street renovated their storefronts to resemble a Bavarian village, an effect that blends nicely with the town's alpine setting. The pretty downtown area has plenty of shops that offer native crafts to those who want mementos of

Mount Robson's icy-blue Berg Glacier rises above beautiful Berg Lake. The glacier occasionally sheds large chunks of ice into the lake.

the trip, and several small motels and restaurants cater to those who decide to stay overnight.

From the moment the *Skeena* leaves Smithers, it is dwarfed by mountains. Magnificent monoliths lie in every direction—vast, ceaseless, mystifying, and occasionally a little threatening. Kathlyn Glacier, a giant slab of ice more than 100 meters thick, is part of the massive landscape. The glacier drains through the picturesque Twin Falls down into the rocky walls of Glacier Gulch. Next, the train crosses a bridge over the turbulent Trout Creek, the first of several dramatic spans along this stretch of track. Paralleling the Buckley River, it travels deep into the ancestral lands of the Carrier, Tsimshian, and Gitxsan peoples. This is a land of misty coastal mountains, thunderous rivers, and ancient traditions.

Just in time to satisfy any cravings for thrills, the *Skeena* soon crosses a series of beautiful, soaring trestles, including the towering Boulder Creek Bridge. At Porphyry Creek, the long curve of the trestle offers an opportunity to take photographs of the front of the train from the rear cars, and at

The Skeena *crosses dozens of rivers as it travels from the Canadian Rockies to the wild and beautiful Pacific Ocean.*

the Mud Creek trestle, stunning views appear on all sides of the train. From high atop rocky ledges, the *Skeena* now embarks on an inspiring four-mile adventure through the magnificent Buckley Canyon. Three tunnels

run through the canyon, including one of the longest used by passenger trains in Canada. You might get a quick glimpse of Buckley Gate, a wall of rock that juts into the river. Below, cliffs compress the Buckley River into a surging flow of white water, and on the opposite bank waterfalls tumble down into the river.

Crossing the Skeena River

The train follows the Buckley River as it emerges from the canyon and carves a path through lush pasturelands. We seem to be the only intruders upon an enormous stretch of wilderness. The highest bridge of the journey is the Sealy Gulch Bridge, at 195 feet, towering over the meeting place of the Buckley and Skeena

Valleys. The canyon walls echo with history as the rapids below roar. Only twelve miles farther, the train crosses its namesake, the Skeena River, for the first of many times. The river and train get their name from the Gitxsan word meaning "river of mists."

As the afternoon passes, the *Skeena* travels through an area known as "the Hazeltons," a cluster of three towns and myriad Indian villages. The train stop at New

Ancient totem poles are common along the route.

Hazelton is a good jumping-off point if you want to explore this area and learn more about the native culture. For centuries, the Gitxsan have maintained communities at the important canyons and junctions of the Skeena River. Within a very small area are eight Gitxsan villages that are home to around 3,500 people. Nearby is the 'Ksan Historical Village and Museum, which preserves and accurately portrays the lifestyles of the people who have always lived here. The replicated village features seven longhouses illustrating many aspects of Gitxsan village life from the distant past. Like its predecessors, 'Ksan's houses form a single line, with each building facing the river so that the large, decorated house fronts and totem poles are visible from the water. First opened in 1959 as the Skeena Treasure House, the museum is the oldest component of the 'Ksan Historical Village and Museum. It was moved in 1970 to its present location near the replicated village. The museum consists of more than 450 ceremonial and utilitarian items.

You may soon realize that you are in a place known as the "Totem Pole Capital of the World," a series of ancient villages where many original totem poles still stand. The Gitxsan tribe is world-renowned for its totem poles, one of which is said to be the oldest in the world. Totem poles have many meanings among the native peoples, and the poles' functions are diverse—some, for example, mark graves, some support roofs, and some celebrate such events as a house moving. The tallest, brightest, and most elaborately carved totem poles often tell of family histories or legends using a complicated series of symbols, often in the form of animals. One of the most respected of the area's totem pole carvers is High Chief Earl Muldon. "In everyday life, these poles are pretty significant," Earl says. "What I've carved in twenty-six years is about fifty totem poles in different sizes, anywhere from six feet to seventy-six feet." Earl has dedicated his life to maintaining the totem pole's importance and presence in the Gitxsan villages. "I'm just trying to re-establish the poles here and make sure people a hundred years from now know that these people had a culture." If you watch carefully from the train, you can occasionally see totem poles from the Hazeltons to Prince Rupert.

Chief Earl Muldon

At this point, we are about four hours from our final destination, and the breathtaking scenery continues as the train follows the Skeena River all the way to Lands' End at the port town of Prince Rupert. This is a good part of the journey to just relax and enjoy the dramatic views. The mighty Skeena River's sheer canyons, high trestles, and foaming green rapids are beautiful, although often mist shrouded. When the mists lift, they reveal the stunning peaks of the surrounding mountains. As the *Skeena* passes through hundreds of miles of isolated wilderness, your thoughts drift to what this land might have been like for the earliest explorers. Beyond the magical glamour of the Wild West lies the hard reality of life in the wilderness.

The trek toward Prince Rupert passes through the dramatic Seven Sisters Range, with pronounced peaks that remain in view for about twenty miles. As the *Skeena* begins a gradual descent to sea level, it continues to follow the Skeena River. Grand glaciers are stretched out atop nearby peaks. Watch carefully as the train passes the abandoned town of Pacific,

notorious for the bears it attracts to its berry flats during the summer. When the train passes through the Kitselas Canyon with its jagged rock outcroppings, the mountains seem to reach right down to the edge of the tracks. Railroad builders were forced to construct four tunnels to get through this area.

In late afternoon, the *Skeena* pulls into Terrace, the final stop before Prince Rupert. With a population of 18,000, Terrace is the largest community between Prince George and Prince Rupert. The center of a large lumbering operation, it is also home to one great fish story, and this one didn't get away. A world-record ninety-two-and-one-half-pound salmon was taken on a rod and reel from the Skeena River near here. Anglers from all over the world make their way to Terrace to try to hook a giant salmon from the Skeena River.

The final stretch into Prince Rupert is among the most scenic parts of the journey. The train crosses the Kitsumkalum River, the first of

The tunnels at Kitselas Canyon were among the most difficult to build.

several tributaries swelling the Skeena River en route to the Pacific Ocean. The mountains of the Kitimat Range border the route on both sides. A stretch of about ten miles features more than fifty waterfalls, some cascading nearly down to trackside. As the river widens near Prince Rupert, numerous little islands dot the Skeena River. The whole scene is breathtaking. "When you come into Prince Rupert," says Anita Marple, "the train is the best because you follow the Skeena River right to the Pacific Ocean, right to the Prince Rupert Harbor. And in all the years I've been going back and forth, there's something new I'll discover, something I hadn't seen before. It's always changing. It is one of the most scenic rail tours in the world."

On the left you can see rustic fishing piers that signal the area where freshwater and salt water begin to mix. At one point, the river widens to nearly a half mile, and harbor seals sometimes frequent this segment of the waterway. The estuary portion of the Skeena River is also the site of tremendous runs of salmon, and the waters are often crowded with fishing boats.

Just before the end of the line, the *Skeena* crosses the bridge over the Zenardi Rapids onto Kaien Island, home of Prince Rupert, and continues past docks and ferry terminals. Finally, the train arrives at the Prince Rupert depot, tucked neatly within a rocky cove. There are a lot of misty days in Prince Rupert—and some that are more than just misty. Even the chamber of commerce has a sense of humor about the weather. They simply call Prince Rupert the "City of Rainbows"—a fine name for a place where incredible journeys end. Some passengers spend a few days in Prince Rupert, others travel on to Alaska or other Canadian wilderness destinations. A few may just head back east on the train.

MATTHEW G. WHEELER

The picturesque city of Prince Rupert at day's end

For the *Skeena* itself, the journey of discovery never ends. Bright and early the next morning, its crew greets another group of excited train adventurers. This village on wheels continues its connection with the rest of Canada, present and past. It turns around and heads back to the mountains and rivers, tunnels and bridges, tracing the paths of the pioneers and of the First Nation's People.

THE TRAIN:
Amtrak's Coast Starlight *offers comfortable economy and first-class accommodations and a range of sleeping berths that suit the needs of individual travelers, couples, and families.*

THE ROUTE:
The Coast Starlight *travels nearly 1,400 miles from Los Angeles, California, to Seattle, Washington.*

DURATION OF THE TRIP:
The Coast Starlight *takes two leisurely days to travel from Los Angeles to Seattle, a total of thirty-six hours on the train, including one overnight on board. More than two dozen stops along the route allow passengers to create any length itinerary they want.*

HIGHLIGHTS:
Amtrak's Coast Starlight *is a romantic ride through some of the West Coast's most beautiful and historic scenery, portions of which cannot be seen except from the train. The trip borders the beaches along the Pacific Ocean, traverses the verdant green of California's fertile interior valley and the northern forests and breathtaking heights of Oregon's Cascade Mountains, before reaching the magnificent Puget Sound.*

The rail adventure on Amtrak's Coast Starlight is a succession of ever-changing scenic experiences, including luxuriously long sections of western landscape that can be seen only from the train.

THE COAST
STAR

A SPECTACULAR PASSAGE ALONG THE EDGE OF the Pacific Ocean, so close to the sparkling blue water that you expect to feel spray from the breaking waves, highlights your first day on the train. The plunging gorges and snowcapped peaks of the misty, densely forested Cascade Mountains of Oregon highlight the second day's trek. In between are some of the most interesting and beautiful places in California, Oregon, and Washington.

As you leave the workaday world behind, you'll be delighted to find that the trip between Los Angeles and Seattle has a tempo and rhythm all its own. You might even want to switch to decaf coffee while you're aboard just to get yourself in sync with the relaxed pace. There is something simple and uncluttered about traveling on long-distance trains. "There's just an ambience," says Tom Buckley, who was born into a railroad family and worked for the railroad most of his life. "There's a romance about rail travel. It's more like a cruise." Your attention to the passage of time dissipates as the rhythm of the rails lulls you into an easygoing mood. Soon you are drawn to mingle with fellow travelers eager to share the joy and romance of the journey. Long-distance trains are no longer the only means of connecting travelers to distant destinations, but they still live on as a unique way to explore vast regions of the country.

In fact, the *Coast Starlight* is Amtrak's attempt to change people's attitudes about their long-distance train routes. "There's always something different; always something exciting," says Amtrak's Charles Roebuck. "We want [people] to enjoy themselves on a memorable occasion, like an anniversary or something like that. Something they never forget, an experience on the *Coast Starlight*."

Today it seems that Amtrak's experiment has been highly successful. The *Coast Starlight* is very popular in the summer months, so if you want to travel during that period you need to book accommodations early. Far less crowded during other months, the train passes through the same countryside, nearly as beautiful even in other seasons. The weather is less predictable, but even that can add to the anticipation. For the trip for the public television production, we took the *Coast Starlight* in December and enjoyed clear weather along the Southern California coastline, rain farther

Union Station in downtown
Los Angeles

north in California, and a dramatic snowstorm that coated the Oregon mountains. Because the *Starlight* is Amtrak's premiere passenger train in the West, the management and staff strive to ensure that it represents the highest standard of quality for rail travel in America. "I think we have the finest scenery of any train ride anywhere in the world," says Gerry Griffo, one of

more than a dozen chiefs of onboard services who work on the *Coast Starlight*. "Our goal is to make the transportation and the service match the beauty and elegance of the scenery that we pass through." The *Coast Starlight* revives the legendary style and elegance of the 1940s "Streamliner Era."

In an effort to create what it calls a premiere "land cruise" travel experience, Amtrak has equipped the *Coast Starlight* route with a Superliner II fleet, some of the newest passenger equipment operating in the country today. Offering first-class and coach accommodations and personal service, Amtrak hopes to re-create the ambience of a cruise ship. Spacious reclining seats, overhead reading lights, wide aisles, and large windows with sweeping views offer guests a relaxing and convenient travel experience.

Los Angeles is the starting point for the *Coast Starlight*'s northbound journey. When you arrive in the City of Angels, you'll discover that it's a lot more than a tangle of freeways. You can easily spend several days touring the abundant sights in the greater metropolitan area. Since the *Coast Starlight* leaves from downtown's Union Station, however, you'll have a great opportunity to explore the heart of Los Angeles, which is often overlooked in favor of Disneyland, Beverly Hills, and Hollywood. Near the station is El Pueblo de Los Angeles Historic Monument, known as the birthplace of the city. California's Spanish heritage comes to life in the enclave's vibrant Mexican marketplace and its simple Avila Adobe, a furnished reconstruction of a one-story adobe house built in 1818.

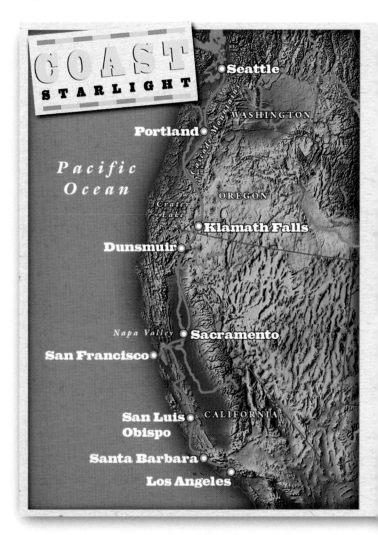

The wraparound picture windows of Amtrak's Sightseer Lounge Car allow guests to enjoy the striking scenic panoramas.

The *Coast Starlight* departs Los Angeles at 9:30 A.M., following the graffiti-covered concrete channel of the Los Angeles River through down-

A tunnel in California's Santa Susanna Mountains.

The Coast Starlight *attempts to create the comfort and magic of the 1940s and 1950s, considered the golden age of passenger rail service in America.*

town. The train makes a brief stop at Glendale, with its 1924 Spanish-style depot and impressive hillside homes. You travel up the broad, heavily populated San Fernando Valley and turn toward the Santa Monica Mountains, which stretch for more than forty miles from the heart of the city west to Point Mugu at the Pacific Ocean. The *Coast Starlight* plunges through a series of tunnels at the scenic Santa Susanna Pass, an area of imposing rock formations and cactus fields. Conjuring up images of bandits chasing the train along this rugged landscape seems natural—the *Lone Ranger* TV series and several western movies were made in this area. Leaving the canyons, the train heads toward the coastal plain, passing through some of the most fertile agricultural areas in the nation. At Oxnard, the hub of this rich agricultural district, the train dashes north through the scenic valley. Crossing the Santa Clara River on a long trestle, you arrive at Ventura, named for the eigtheenth-century San Buenaventura Mission, which stands just to the right of the tracks. Here you catch your first sight of the Pacific Ocean.

A LINK TO THE PAST:
THE SPANISH MISSIONS

One of California's strongest connections to its past is found in the string of Spanish missions that stretch from San Diego to San Francisco, and the route of the

Dan Krieger

Coast Starlight traces much of the old mission road, El Camino Real—the "Royal Road." Several missions can be seen from the windows of the train, and some of the most interesting missions are within easy reach of stops along the route. Glimpsing the old missions from the train offers a sense of what life might have been like along this path more than two centuries ago.

In 1769 Spain's highest-ranking official in Mexico sent a Sacred Expedition to establish mission colonies in what was called Upper California. Led by Father Junípero Serra, the purpose of the expedition was to convert the Indians and gain a foothold against possible Russian and English expansion. Father Serra established nine missions, and twelve others were built later. The missions were specifically located so there would only be a day's journey by horseback between them. All twenty-one missions survive today.

At Ventura, the Coast Starlight passes by the San Buenaventura Mission. A pretty garden sits next to the whitewashed and red-tiled church. The restored church was the only California mission to use wooden bells, which are now preserved at the Mission Museum along with other items. Just one stop farther up the coast, the historic Santa Barbara Mission can be seen from the train as it leaves the city. Built of native sandstone, the mission church rests in a beautiful natural setting between the coastline and the Santa Ynez Mountains. Dubbed the "Queen of the Missions," it is one of the best preserved and most unique examples of mission architecture, the only one in California to employ a twin-tower design. A lovely fountain in front of the build-

The Coast Starlight *route passes the Mission San Miguel Arcángel.*

ing is fed by an aqueduct built by the Indians in 1808. The aqueduct also irrigates a beautiful garden in the cemetery next to the church.

The Mission San Luis Obispo de Tolosa was founded in 1772 by Padre Junípero Serra. Although early missions had reed roofs, these proved vulnerable to fire so the missionary priests turned to fireproof red tiles like those used in their native Spain. The Mission San Luis Obispo was the first to make extensive use of these red tiles, which have become identified with the California mission style. A museum here highlights the Indian, Spanish,

PHOTO BY TERRY RUSCIN

Mexican, and American periods of California history, and a gift shop provides mementos reminiscent of those early days and diverse cultures.

At San Miguel, the Coast Starlight passes close by the Mission San Miguel Arcangle, which appears today much as it did in the eighteenth century. Founded in 1797, it has the best maintained interior of all California missions, full of intricate painting and decoration. Dan Krieger, a professor of history at California Polytech at San Luis Obispo, is an ardent admirer of this historical monument. "It's one of the only nearly unrestored missions in California. Much of it is original. It's a spectacular place," Krieger says. "The altar itself is the most spectacular of all of the altars in the California mission churches." Full of fanciful color and design, it also bears a three-dimensional "seeing eye of God" that juts out above it, signifying that God sees all, God knows all. "It was a very effective teaching tool," says Krieger.

Most California missions went out of use by the mid-1800s, only to make a comeback decades later with tourists. "In the 1880s, as the railroad came through here, people began to undergo what we call 'mission mania'," says Krieger. Today, the Coast Starlight is a perfect way to discover the romantic past of California's mission era.

The interior of the Mission San Miguel Arcángel.

Cool ocean breezes bear the refreshing scent of the sea as the *Coast Starlight* hugs the California coastline for the next four hours. From the train are views of what is arguably one of the most scenic stretches of

The Coast Starlight *edges along the beautiful California coastline.*

rail landscape in America. "One of the things that surprised me is how close we come to the ocean," exclaims a wide-eyed passenger. For more than a hundred miles, the route travels along the beach. Because of the restricted access to Vandenberg Air Force Base and two large, private ranches, the train provides the only way to see much of this coastal country. Although nearly all of California's 1,100-mile shoreline is alluring, the south-central coast is a place of rare beauty. The first part of this ocean-side voyage is a thirty-mile expanse between Ventura and Santa Barbara where the tracks rest on a narrow shelf between the ocean and the mountains. For miles the *Coast Starlight* glides along sandy beaches and rocky shorelines. During part of this stretch, the rails parallel Route 1, the old Pacific Coast Highway, and you can see the seawall built to protect the road and the tracks.

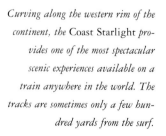

Curving along the western rim of the continent, the Coast Starlight *provides one of the most spectacular scenic experiences available on a train anywhere in the world. The tracks are sometimes only a few hundred yards from the surf.*

As the morning sun brightens, the *Coast Starlight* passes several ocean-front communities in this area. First among these is the resort town of Carpinteria, with an excellent beach that is considered a great vacation spot for families. Centuries ago, the Chumash Indians established a settlement

here because nearby tar pits provided waterproof caulking material for their seagoing canoes. It was their boat-building skills that led the Spanish to call the area *La Carpinteria,* or "the carpentry shop." Farther along, "exposed" sunbathers are sometimes seen as the train passes the appropriately named resort community of Summerland, and then the picturesque beach community of Miramar signals the train's approach to Santa Barbara. A lagoon to the left of the train is a bird refuge and centerpiece of the Santa

The Coast Starlight *passes a number of exclusive beach communities.*

Barbara Zoological Gardens. The *Coast Starlight* arrives in charming, historic Santa Barbara just after noon. To the left of the station stands a city landmark. The old Moreton Bay fig tree, planted in 1877, has branches that spread 160 feet. It is considered the largest tree of its kind in the United States.

Beyond this astounding specimen lie bougainvillea-covered adobe walls, red-tile roofs, and palm-lined streets and beaches. Together these make Santa Barbara one of the prettiest beach communities in California. Whether you drive here from Los Angeles before boarding the *Coast Starlight*—it takes about two hours—or make this your first off-train excursion, Santa Barbara is a place to spend some time, and you can start your visit right from the train station. Walking tours feature beautiful homes, historic buildings, lovely gardens, and graceful boulevards. The 1929 County Courthouse, known for its magnificent Spanish Revival architecture, typifies the image Santa Barbara reflects since the 1925 earthquake. The Santa Barbara Historical Society Museum and El Presidio de Santa Barbara State Historical Park offer several excellent examples of adobe structures. An undeniable centerpiece of the community's Hispanic past, the beautiful Mission Santa Barbara features twin sandstone towers. The design dates from 27 B.C. and was adapted by the padres from an illustration they found in a book of Roman architecture. Although the mission was founded in 1786, the present church and buildings were not completed until 1820. Sitting on a high promontory, the mission can easily be seen from the train as the *Coast Starlight* resumes its journey northward.

Rolling along the edge of the continent, the train curves past driftwood-strewn beaches, high bluffs, secluded coves, rocky tidal pools, and sand dunes. For the next three hours, the clear blue California sky blends seamlessly with the lucent blue ocean as the train skirts atop seawalls overlooking the frothy surf. As the *Coast Starlight* cuts a path between mountains and ocean, the trip between Santa Barbara and San Luis Obispo is a time to sit back and appreciate the glorious vistas along the

BRIAN SOLOMON

Pacific Ocean. It is the perfect opportunity to enjoy lunch in the windowed dining car or have a sandwich served at your seat or in your private sleeping car. "One of the most intriguing things about eating in the dining car on the train, besides the quality of the food and, of course, the scenery, is that it's one of the last places that still practices community seating," says Amtrak's Gerry Griffo. "You are apt to sit with anybody on board the train

at your meal, and it always makes for exciting and interesting conversation."

As the train climbs from Santa Barbara you can spot on the horizon the islands that define the Santa Barbara Channel. On clear days the Channel Islands seem close enough to touch. Of the eight islands in all, Anacapa Island is the closest at just

Since there are no roads or trails along much of this part of the coastline, the train provides a scenic perspective not otherwise available.

Crossing a trestle over one of the many beautiful beaches that dot the route.

eleven miles offshore. The fragile and beautiful environment of these islands provides refuge for rare species of plants and animals that exist nowhere else. Often called America's own Galapagos, they are home to one of the nation's richest marine environments.

Passing over Jalama Beach on a high trestle, the rails soon bend around Point Conception, an elbow along the California coastline where ocean currents collide, creating treacherous maritime conditions. After Jalama Beach, the *Coast Starlight* enters Vandenberg Air Force Base, with its long stretches of secluded beaches rarely seen by travelers. Largely undeveloped, this striking area features broad sandy beaches framed by high coastal bluffs easily viewed from the train.

From Point Conception, the tracks continue west but begin to turn slightly to the north, reaching Point Arguello, another dangerous spot for coastal mariners. It is easy to be deceived by the beauty and apparent serenity of this place, but in truth the rocky reefs at Point Arguello have been the site of many shipwrecks over the years. The isolated Point Arguello Lighthouse sits on a jutting cliff and marks this treacherous section of coast. But even the legendary beacon and its powerful fog siren could not prevent several ships, including the *Santa Rosa* in 1911, from being lost on the rocks in the heavy fog. This is one of California's most difficult lighthouses to reach, and the train is one of the best ways to observe it. Migrating whales can be seen from this vantage point in the spring and fall.

The tracks continue through Vandenberg, crossing the Santa Ynez River at Surf. At Point Purisima the *Coast Starlight* begins to leave the broad coastal terrace and head inland, threading through Schuman Canyon and passing Guadalupe and the Santa Maria Valley, another rich agricultural district. In Guadalupe, be sure to take note of the beautiful mission to the right of the tracks.

At Pismo Beach, you get a final view of the blue Pacific Ocean. This popular resort town is famous for Pismo clams, the wide beach, and the massive sand dunes that can be seen on the left side of the train. The Nipomo Dunes create an eight-mile playground of giant, natural sandcastles perfect for birdwatching, horseback riding, and hiking. After Pismo Beach, the *Coast Starlight* leaves the Pacific for good, slowing winding through the hills of the Santa Lucia Range to the town of San Luis Obispo.

This quaint, central California community lies twelve miles inland from the ocean in the center of an expansive agricultural region. Around mid-afternoon the *Coast Starlight* arrives at the attractive 1934 depot. Especially in the summer months, the train provides an ideal way to visit San Luis Obispo because the streets are very congested with cars and tourists. Just about everything in town is within walking distance of the train station, and you'll avoid the issues of parking and snags in the traffic. Shops, restaurants, and a variety of accommodations make the town an easy place to spend a night before reboarding the *Coast Starlight* the next afternoon.

Originally founded as Mission San Luis Obispo de Tolosa, the town is also a popular starting point for those wishing to explore the scenic central coast of California. Within easy reach are Morro Bay, Pismo Beach, San Simeon, lighthouses, and local wineries—and the fabulous Hearst Castle, the extravagant home of the late newspaper magnate William Randolph Hearst. "Hearst Castle is really the last of the great estates that were constructed during a period in American history called the Gilded Age," says James Allen, Hearst Castle public affairs officer. "It is the largest to come into public hands with its collections, its decorative and fine art, its furnishings and paintings still intact." Built over a thirty-year period, the estate was completed in 1947 and encompasses a 130-room main house, guest houses, pools, and acres of gardens.

BRIAN SOLOMON

The Golden Gate Bridge, one of the world's best known landmarks, is among the magical views of San Francisco available on the route of the Coast Starlight.

Leaving San Luis Obispo, the *Coast Starlight* crosses an old trestle and climbs toward Cuesta Pass and a superlative railroading adventure. Rounding two spectacular horseshoe curves, it is possible to catch a glimpse of the entire train wrapped around the loop. Monolithic rock formations create dazzling views as the train ascends 1,300 feet into the Santa Lucia Range. Over the next eleven miles, a trip of a half hour, the *Starlight* passes through several tunnels while climbing the mountainside. The wild scenery typifies why the *Coast Starlight* is such a unique and romantic train experience and adds to the unforgettable nature of the journey. Emerging from the 3,616-foot summit tunnel, the train and its enchanted passengers descend to Santa Margarita and enter a region of rolling hills.

Here the dominant color of the landscape changes from blue to green, as ocean vistas are replaced by lush, verdant fields. During the late after-

The Coast Starlight *cuts through the verdant green of California's fertile interior valley.*

noon, the *Coast Starlight* streaks northward, passing the pretty town of Paso Robles, which in Spanish means "the pass of the oaks." Not long after passing San Miguel, home to yet another beautiful mission, the train parallels the Salinas River, entering the 450-mile-long Central Valley, an agricultural area known as the nation's "Salad Bowl." Giant fields of lettuce, broccoli, lima beans, and sugar beets line the tracks.

Around 6:15 P.M., the *Coast Starlight* makes a brief stop at the Salinas station, where Amtrak provides motor coach connections to the nearby resort communities of Monterey and Carmel. Salinas is also the jumping-off point for anyone interested in exploring the area that influenced Nobel Prize–winning author John Steinbeck while he was growing up. This area is the main setting for some of Steinbeck's most popular novels, including

East of Eden, Of Mice and Men, and *Tortilla Flat.* Steinbeck called *East of Eden* "a sort of autobiography of the Salinas Valley." The book covers more than fifty years and three generations of families living in Salinas. The Steinbeck House, a Victorian structure where the author was born in 1902, is now a restaurant in Salinas. Nearby King City, where Steinbeck's father was the first railroad agent, is also a setting in several of his novels. Steinbeck drew inspiration from this land and remained connected to it throughout his life. After winning the Nobel Prize in 1962, he wrote to a friend, "This prize business is only different from the Lettuce Queen of Salinas in degree."

As nighttime descends, the *Coast Starlight* reaches the San Francisco/Oakland area. Even in darkness, you can see the impressive Bay Bridge out the left windows of the train, spanning San Francisco Bay and linking Oakland and San Francisco. You pass through the heavily industrialized district of Oakland before arriving at the Amtrak station located at Jack London Square, Oakland's renovated waterfront dining and shopping district. The First and Last Chance Saloon, a favorite hangout of the author Jack London, is within walking distance of the station. Oakland and the next stop at Emeryville provide bus connections into San Francisco for passengers wishing to spend time exploring the Bay Area.

The *Coast Starlight* heads farther inland during the night. Most passengers have turned in as the train makes the trip to Sacramento, California's capital and its largest inland city. The train arrives in Sacramento around midnight. Located one block from the Amtrak station is the California State Railroad Museum. Considered the largest interpretative railroad museum in the world, it occupies four buildings and includes twenty-one restored locomotives and railroad cars. Rail fans with extra time may wish to disembark here and visit the museum in the morning.

Amtrak's new station in Oakland, California, is located in the heart of Jack London Square, the city's waterfront district named for the famous writer.

THE NAPA VALLEY WINE TRAIN

One of the most popular side trips from the Coast Starlight's Oakland stop is an exploration of California wine country, and for train buffs, the Napa Valley Wine Train adds an extra bonus. "Everybody that takes this trip really enjoys it," says Vincent De Domenico, entrepreneur, innovator of Rice-a-Roni, and managing partner of the Wine Train. "We set out to be even better than the Orient Express in Europe," he says. "I like good food and good wine, and the idea is you want to combine the two because they really fit together."

COURTESY NAPA VALLEY WINE TRAIN

The Napa Valley Wine Train is a three-hour, thirty-six-mile excursion through one of the world's most famous wine valleys. This brief rail adventure offers a return to the gracious era of elegant rail travel and distinguished service. The train's beautifully restored Champagne Vista Dome Car, appointed with high-backed chairs, capitalizes on the surrounding scenery. Its lavishly restored 1917 vintage Pullman dining car features polished wood, fine fabrics, and etched glass.

While the scenery and the train provide a unique and wonderful "dining room," the highlight of this trip is the excellent California cuisine and the wine tasting. "Our wine list is representative of the valley—it's very diverse," says knowledgeable wine educator Brent Trojan, "so hopefully there's a wine . . . for everybody on board." Experienced wine lovers and newcomers alike feel at ease tasting wine in the comfortable lounge cars. Nearby, Chef Patrick Finney crafts creative California cuisine in his rolling kitchen. "We are capable of serving about 135 gourmet meals in about thirty-five minutes," he says. "While our menu is not as extensive as a free-standing restaurant, what we do we do very well."

COURTESY NAPA VALLEY WINE TRAIN

This leisurely day of good wine and food on board the Napa Valley Wine Train is a lavish digression but a highly worthwhile enhancement of your Coast Starlight adventure.

During the night the *Coast Starlight* travels the length of the magnificent Sacramento Valley, hemmed in on three sides by giant mountain ranges. The moonlight reflecting off these rugged peaks creates evocative images. Through the heart of these mountains lie the twelve million acres of the flat, open Sacramento Valley. Along with the San Joaquin Valley to the south, they form one of the most fertile production regions on earth. As the train leaves the Sacramento Valley and heads into the foothills of the Cascade Range, early risers may catch glimpses of the moonlit Shasta Lake. Soon the landscape becomes more rugged as the train follows the winding course of the Sacramento River into the historic railroad town of Dunsmuir, nestled in the foothills of 14,162-foot Mount Shasta. "You can't live in Dunsmuir without knowing the railroad is here. You hear it every day," says Ron McCloud, who brought his family here from San Francisco for a simpler life. "You feel the ground shake sometimes when the heavy freight trains go through. The town is here because of the railroad."

Established in the 1880s when the rail line was built through the Upper Sacramento River Valley, the original town was called Pusher and was located about a mile from the current town site. It got its name because extra engines were needed to push the train up the steep canyon. The town moved to its present location and was renamed Dunsmuir in 1886. It served as a major railroad center for the Southern Pacific until the 1950s, when the introduction of diesel trains cut the workforce in half and reduced the town's population from 5,000 to the roughly 2,000 people who live in Dunsmuir today. The town is now a delightful tourist haven with excellent fishing in the summer and skiing in the winter. Most passengers are still asleep as the train pulls out of Dunsmuir in the pre-dawn hours and continues north.

As daylight breaks on the second day of the journey, the *Coast Starlight* rumbles through a tunnel before crossing the border from California into Oregon. "Ladies and gentlemen, a very pleasant good morning," greets Gerry Griffo on the train PA system. "We trust you all spent a very pleas-

Ron McCloud

The breathtaking heights of the northern forests of Oregon's Cascade Mountains provide a dramatic contrast to earlier coastal scenes.

ant night on board the *Coast Starlight*. We'd like to let you know that breakfast is being served in our dining car. Plenty of fresh hot coffee, pancakes, and eggs, just the way you like them." As the morning sun warms the land, a hearty breakfast warms the body and beautiful new vistas are food for the soul. A new day of the *Coast Starlight*'s journey begins, and you are in for equally spectacular but completely different scenery.

Shortly after entering Oregon and winding its way through the beautiful Cascade Mountains, the *Coast Starlight* passes the town of Klamath Falls, at an elevation of 4,105 feet. Just north of town, the train reaches the eastern shore of Upper Klamath Lake, which it follows for eighteen miles. One of the largest bodies of fresh water west of the Rockies, Upper Klamath Lake is home to snow-white pelicans, which can be seen on the lake in great numbers between April and September.

High mountain peaks surround the tracks throughout this region. Mount McLoughlin, at 9,760 feet, is visible across the lake. Soon, however, the summit disappears from view as the tracks swing away from the lake at Chiloquin and follow the Williamson River for the next fifteen miles. Several giant peaks off to the left frame Crater Lake, the deepest lake in the nation and arguably Oregon's most famous tourist attraction. The *Coast Starlight* is a great way to visit Crater Lake and the remote Cascade wilderness areas of south-central Oregon. Around 9:30 A.M., the northbound train arrives at the town of Chemult, gateway to Crater Lake.

Crater Lake was formed more than 7,700 years ago when the 12,000-foot Mount Mazama exploded, a blast forty-two times more powerful than the 1980 eruption of Mount St. Helens in Washington State. As the 5,000-foot mountaintop collapsed, it formed a *caldera,* or basin. Lava flow sealed the bottom, allowing the volcanic crater to fill with water from centuries of rainfall and snowmelt and creating the 1,932-foot-deep lake, the ninth deepest in the world. Legends of Native peoples who inhabited this part of

Wizard Island punctuates the deep blue waters of Crater Lake.

Oregon thousands of years ago indicate that they likely witnessed the terrifying explosion that formed Crater Lake. Some of the legends tell of a battle between two powerful gods that resulted in the eruption. The result of this fearful event is a masterpiece of natural beauty, one of the most stunningly beautiful sites in the United States. Crater Lake's most dramatic feature is the remarkably clear sapphire blue color of its water. At sunrise, the tranquil blue pool of water seems almost otherworldly.

Shortly after leaving Chemult, the *Coast Starlight* makes a sharp turn to the west, heading over the heart of the Cascade Mountains for a three-hour trek that is one of this journey's most exhilarating scenic delights. Striking views open to the right as the train follows beautiful Odell Lake for four miles, and ahead

The Coast Starlight *emerges from a tunnel in the Cascade Range of southern Oregon.*

of the train rise the inspiring vistas of the Cascade Range. The beauty of this pristine wilderness is incomparable as the route gradually ascends to the 4,840-foot Cascade Summit, offering views that can be seen only from the train. Peacefulness envelops the *Coast Starlight* as it moves along the tracks beneath massive trees so high they create their own natural tunnel. It is easy to feel small meandering through these towering forests. Daylight pierces through to create dramatic effects in the deep woods. During the trip to tape the public television program, a snowstorm blanketed the forest to create a wondrous winterland. "Yesterday morning, palm trees and sunshine," exclaimed one passenger. "This morning, snow! It's just a beautiful trip."

Soon the *Coast Starlight* crosses the divide of the Cascade Mountains at Willamette Pass and begins a dramatic descent of more than 3,500 feet in the next fifty miles. The path downward along twisting switchback tracks is one of the most scenic mountain train routes in the country. Numerous tunnels pierce the densely forested slopes, and waterfalls tumble down the ravines. The *Starlight* itself clings to the side of the steep cliffs of the

canyon wall. While the light snow during our trip added to the magic of the Cascade Mountain experience, this area is known for *lots* of snowfall. Some of the tunnels the train passes through are actually snow sheds built to protect the tracks from snow accumulations and avalanches. The jutting peaks of the Cascade Range provide a dramatic backdrop for the colorful vegetation of the Willamette National Forest. If you keep your eyes on the forest edge, an occasional elk or deer can sometimes be glimpsed not far from trackside.

During the afternoon, the *Coast Starlight* enters the Willamette Valley—Oregon's wine country. The wet temperate trough between the Cascade and Coast Ranges is a nearly perfect climate for growing grapes for pinot noir and chardonnay. More than sixty wineries dot the Willamette Valley, and many Oregon varietals are considered among the best wines in the world. "Good afternoon, ladies and gentlemen. It is wine-tasting time again," announces Charles Roebuck, another of the chiefs of onboard services on the *Coast Starlight*. "If you're traveling in our sleeping accommodation, now is the time to come down and taste champagne with us in our Pacific lounge car. We know you will enjoy yourself and love the wine that we're serving today here on the *Coast Starlight* train." A wine-tasting reception, featuring selections from California, Oregon, and Washington, is a part of the *Coast Starlight*'s first-class service.

Charles Roebuck serving wine to passengers

As passengers relax with their champagne, the *Coast Starlight* makes only two stops on the way to Portland: at Salem, Oregon's second largest city and the state capital, and at Albany, a charming river town with more than 700 historic buildings. For several miles, the train passes through small agricultural communities as the tracks travel directly through the town centers. Approaching the suburbs of Portland, we cross the Clackamas River. On clear days, you can see Mount Hood off to the right, towering at 11,235 feet.

OREGON TOURISM/BOB POOL PHOTO

Only an hour's drive from Portland, the beautiful and seemingly serene Mount Hood is believed to be an active volcano.

While the scheduled stop of just thirty-five minutes at Portland's Union Station isn't long enough to see much of the area, people with a full day to spend usually head for the spectacular beauty of the seventy-five-mile-long Columbia River Gorge, within easy reach of Portland along the Columbia River Scenic Highway. The road takes you literally to the doorstep of the major points of interest, including dozens of waterfalls. The highlight is Multnomah Falls; at 620 feet, it's the second highest waterfall in the United States. It tumbles in two tiers down the gorge, adding to the natural drama of this rugged terrain. A rushing ribbon of water pours over the top of the ridge into a stone pool before spilling over to form a second, lower falls. A paved path leads to a bridge overlooking the lower falls with good views of the upper falls.

Leaving Portland, the train follows the Willamette River through an industrial section of the city before crossing the Columbia River, which forms the border between Oregon and Washington. This mighty river, America's second longest, has a total navigable length of 2,136 miles. In the midst of the river is Hayden Island, with vessels and dockside facilities that support the vast shipping industry. On the opposite bank is Vancouver, Washington, the oldest continuous settlement in the Northwest, established as a fort in 1825 by the Hudson's Bay Company. We follow the Columbia River for a stretch of about forty miles to

Mount Hood looms over the Portland skyline.

Longview, where the river heads west to the Pacific Ocean and the train turns north. If the weather if clear, you can see Mount St. Helens off to the right shortly after leaving Longview. Its spectacular eruption in 1980 sent ash in this direction.

...he *Coast Starlight* follows the old stagecoach ... Seattle, meandering past farms and logging ..., the train pulls into Olympia, the capital of ... southernmost end of Puget Sound. Above ...ne Nisqually River and follows Puget Sound, ... and entering a nauti-...ainder of the trip. For ...e panorama includes ...secluded fishing coves ...line of Puget Sound. ...na, watch for excellent ...orthwest's greatest ...lly snowcapped Mount

The Seattle skyline frames the south-bound Coast Starlight.

...owering 14,410 feet, with twenty-six glaciers ...n easy day trip from Seattle, the national park ...cellent driving and hiking trails that offer great ...w, however, passengers must feast only on more ...*rlight* makes a brief stop in Tacoma. Afterward, ...ur amazing journey. The ninety-minute jaunt ...of your glorious two-day adventure. Seattle, ...ngton and Puget Sound, is the largest city of ...n important seaport. As the train arrives at King ...f the Olympic Range provide a striking back-...le skyline.

...oyed the wonderful geographic extremes of California and the Pacific Northwest. While there are many wonderful places to stop and much fascinating history along the route of this journey, the true joy of this trip is the ever changing landscapes—soaring mountains, green valleys, thick forests, jagged cliffs, and pristine beaches—enjoyed from the peaceful perspective of the train. "People have a whole range of emotions about the train," says Amtrak's Scott Hurd. "For a lot of them, it's something romantic. If they're a train buff, there's something about riding the train that they love. You get people who are doing it just for the experience, just seeing the country and getting out and just kind of joyriding."

The *Coast Starlight* is one heck of a joyride.

Scott Hurd

Trip Profile

THE TRAIN:

The American Orient Express is a private luxury train with restored cars reminiscent of trains of the 1940s and 1950s. The train includes two dining cars, three lounge cars, and a variety of sleeping accommodations.

THE ROUTE:

Beginning in New Orleans and ending in Washington, D.C., this trip of nearly 1,400 miles passes through eight states, with stops at Savannah, Charleston, and Richmond.

DURATION OF THE TRIP:

This seven-day trip makes stops each day at major southern cities. Passengers spend six nights sleeping on board the train.

HIGHLIGHTS:

The train travels through remote areas of the South, including the seldom-seen marshlands bordering the Gulf of Mexico. Passengers have full days of sight-seeing in some of the region's most historic cities, discovering the romance and culture of the Old—and new—South.

The Deep South. The Old South. The Antebellum South. Each phrase conjures up impressions of the American South. "There's an image of moonlight and magnolias and big houses and everybody's working in the fields," says folklorist Nick Spitzer. "That's the idyllic image, the Stephen Foster image."

THE AMERIC

IT IS AN INVITING PICTURE, BUT ONE THAT CLASHES with the realities of other southern images. "It is hard to celebrate slavery," says Spitzer. "I don't think you celebrate moonlight and magnolias and ignore the lack of human freedom that the Old South was built on." For many people, especially those from other parts of the country, the South can appear to be a place frozen in time, almost stuck in its past. History and tradition are very important here, even as life and conditions change. Much of that history and tradition, and the beauty of the South, is found in its oldest cities and at other stops along the railroad tracks traveled in the making of "The American South by Rail" television program for PBS.

Our southern rail adventure begins along the Mississippi River Delta in New Orleans, Louisiana. Famous for Mardi Gras, music, and food, the "Big Easy" is a great place to spend time before boarding the train. While

AN SOUTH
BY RAIL

The American Orient Express *offers rail tours to all corners of the United States and Canada.*

most tourists head for the famed French Quarter, a truly unique New Orleans experience can be found only a few blocks away at the French Market. A New Orleans institution since 1790, today it is a place where local residents and tourists mingle with chefs in search of distinctive New Orleans ingredients. "I wonder if I could sample some of the smoked alligator on a stick," Anthony Hubbard asks a French Market vendor. "New Orleans is a wonderful town, a great city, an old city, very classic. It's a lot of fun," says Anthony, the executive chef on the *American Orient Express.* "I enjoy coming here every single time."

On the morning the train departed, our television crew joined chef Anthony on a trip to the French Market. "Any chef you ask would love to come to New Orleans," he says. "You have Creole food. You have Cajun food. Both are very old and still very contemporary, and this is a hotbed of that type of food." Anthony is here to buy food that his staff will use to prepare virtually all of our meals over the next week. "I think I'd like to buy fifteen of these," he says, pointing to a basket of fresh crabs. "We are going on a seven-day trip from New Orleans to Washington, D.C. We have eighty-five passengers who are going to be eating a lot of food, so I'm looking to find some of the special ingredients that I can only find in New Orleans." In addition to crabs, Anthony picks up Louisiana bay leaves, toasted nuts, and fresh pears, leaving with several bags of goodies. "On the *American Orient Express,* we consider our food and our service five star and part of that is getting the best possible quality to our passengers. And what that means for me is going out and finding the fresh-est and best ingredients that the area I'm in has to offer. And here in New Orleans, the French Market is the place for those ingredients."

While Anthony prepares the kitchen, the crew puts the final touches on the rest of the train as passengers arrive for an early evening reception and dinner on board. "You're in Cabin 8," a porter says, greeting an arriv-ing couple. "Go on up there, and I'll show you to your cabin." Our trip through the South is on board the *American Orient Express,* a pri-vate luxury train that offers rail excursions throughout the country. For some passengers, this is their first train vacation. For oth-ers, it is their first trip through the American South. "I've been trying to set myself in that time period, putting myself in the antebellum gown and the big garden hat and all of that," says passenger Ruth Goldfarb, who came to America from Germany in 1936 at the age of six. "The first movie I saw was *Gone with the Wind,* and it made a tremendous impression on me," she says. "It'll be exciting to see what it is like in reality."

Chef Anthony Hubbard at the French Market in New Orleans

After its passengers enjoy a good night's sleep while the train is parked at the Amtrak station, the *American Orient Express* pulls out of New Orleans in the early morning, heading east. The moisture in the air mixes with the heat of the morning sun to create a glistening radiance as the engine heads directly into the rising sun. Early risers enjoy the beauty and quiet of morning on the train and the sheen of the passing landscape. The *AOE* offers passengers two choices for breakfast: a continental breakfast set up in

The grassy marshlands of Louisiana.

the lounge cars or a full breakfast served in the dining car. The first leg of the trip is from New Orleans to the port city of Mobile, Alabama, a short jaunt that takes about two hours.

Water is a dominant characteristic of this trek through southern Louisiana and coastal Mississippi, an exotic land of steamy swamps, endless marshes, and moss-covered trees. The morning sun bounces off the sparkling water as the train crosses a channel connecting giant Lake Pontchartrain with the Mississippi River. When the *AOE* passes through the Bayou Savage National Wildlife Refuge, passengers can see barges and other ships making their way along the Intercoastal Waterway to the Gulf of Mexico. "I think trains are an amazing way to see the landscape," says Nick Spitzer, a folklorist at the University of New Orleans. "It's especially true here because they've built up a grade through what is essentially a floating marsh. The views are all water vistas, swamp vistas, bayous, canals, and even the open Gulf on occasion. It's kind of a liquid land environment." Watch the water for occasional houses on stilts and, off in the distance, giant oil platforms. As the train crosses a two-mile trestle over the entrance to St. Louis Bay, you can see the Mississippi Sound, a place where pelicans and great blue herons sometimes fly. If you watch carefully, you may spot an alligator in the marshy wetlands along the route.

The train follows the flat marshlands through the picturesque Gulf Coast communities of Pass Christian, Gulfport, and Biloxi, an area beautifully described in John Grisham's best-selling novel *The Pelican Brief:* "The

Folklorist Nick Spitzer

marshlands were a marvel of natural evolution. Using the rich sediment as food, they grew into a green paradise of cypress and oak and dense patches of pickerelweed and bulrush and cattails. The water was filled with crawfish, shrimp, oysters, red snapper, flounder, pompano, bream, crabs, and alligators. The coastal plain was a sanctuary for wildlife. Hundreds of species of migratory birds came to roost."

AN AMTRAK ALTERNATIVE

The fixed itinerary and cost of the American Orient Express *may lead some travelers to look at other options for exploring the South by rail.*

Luckily, several Amtrak trains provide more modestly priced alternatives to the route used by the AOE. Amtrak's Crescent, *for instance, travels from New Orleans to Washington, D.C., on a westerly route through Georgia, the Carolinas, and Virginia. It misses the cities of Savannah and Charleston, however, so one of Amtrak's Silver Service trains—the Silver Meteor, the Silver Palm, or the Silver Star—may provide a more appealing choice. With onboard dining and sleeping accommodations, these trains continue the long history of passenger rail travel service between the Northeast and Florida. All three Silver Service trains run between New York and Miami, with many destinations in between, and all three operate daily in both directions. It is easy to create a personalized itinerary that allows you to explore any of the stops along the route. The Silver Meteor most closely resembles the route taken in "The American South by Rail." It departs from New York City with stops in Washington, D.C., Richmond, Savannah, and Charleston before its final destination of Miami.*

If you are interested in adding some stops at smaller southern towns as well as the main stops, try the Silver Palm. Additional stops at Wilson and Fayetteville in North Carolina, Dillon and Florence in South Carolina, and Jessup in Georgia are among the places you might explore. At Dillon, Amtrak provides connecting motorcoach service to Myrtle Beach. One excellent way to explore much of the history of the South is to buy a round-trip ticket for the route between Washington and Charleston and add different stops to your itinerary as you travel south and north.

While Amtrak can't match the luxury and service of the AOE, it does provide easy access to the major cities of the South.

©AMTRAK

Grisham's novel depicts how much of this area changed with the discovery of oil, and, indeed, thousands of acres of coastal marshes have been lost to development. For those who have never seen this part of America, however, the marsh is still a mysterious spectacle.

Wonderful views of the watery environment surround the train as it passes through seldom-seen stretches of the Gulf Coast. This seems like a place apart from the rest of America. "This is the central Gulf Coast," Nick

The Mobile, Alabama, skyline

Spitzer says. "I like to say it's south of the South. It's deeper than the Deep South. It's more connected to the Caribbean in a lot of ways, culturally. Physically, it's different, too, because it's very low land. It is the river lowland of the Mississippi Valley coming to

the Gulf of Mexico." Spitzer, who is host of the *American Routes* series on public radio, says this is often an overlooked area of the country. "A lot of Americans think of the East Coast and the West Coast. They forget that there's a south coast, a third coast, as I like to call it—the Gulf Coast. The core of the Gulf Coast is really this stretch between New Orleans and Mobile," he says. "There's no better movie, whether it's PBS or CBS, than just looking out the window of a train and watching the land and the people go by."

The train crosses the Mississippi-Alabama line as the tracks mingle with several small creeks nearing Mobile. The busy docks on the right signal the maritime importance of Mobile. As the *American Orient Express*

The Azalea Trail Maids welcome the AOE to Mobile.

slowly pulls into the Amtrak station at about nine in the morning, a half-dozen brightly dressed young women provide a southern welcome that seems out of another era. The cheerful girls are wearing brightly colored ruffled dresses and crinolines, large brimmed hats, and white gloves. These are the Azalea Trail Maids, high school seniors who are chosen and trained as ambassadors of goodwill to Mobile's growing number of visitors. They often welcome special groups to town and are here this morning to greet the passengers of the *American Orient Express*. The group draws its name from the fact that more than fifty varieties of azaleas bloom each spring in Mobile, making it the Azalea Capital of the World.

Much like the train route you have just traveled, Mobile is a city connected to the water. Located at the north end of the twenty-seven-mile Mobile Bay, it is a leading Gulf Coast seaport. The French first settled Mobile in 1704, and the city's early wealth and importance were directly related to its location on the water. Today Mobile is a graceful city noted for its charming boulevards lined with giant moss-draped live oaks. "Mobile some years ago was referred to as America's best-kept secret. But that is no longer the case," says resident Velma Croom. "It's a unique city. It is extremely southern. It is very proud of its past." Velma Croom speaks about Mobile with the knowledge of someone who has lived here all her life. "This tiny frontier settlement was the first capital of the French empire in the New World and the port of entry of the entire Louisiana Territory," she says. "As visitors come into Mobile, the reconstructed Fort Conde [is] a wonderful place to start a tour. It is a replica of the original French fort built in 1704." Another popular attraction is Battleship Park, where the battleship *Alabama* and the submarine *Drum* are moored and opened for tours. Mobile has preserved much of its past with more than 4,000 buildings on the National Register

MOBILE CONVENTION & VISITORS CORPORATION

An ornate cast iron fountain sits at the center of Bienville Square in downtown Mobile.

of Historic Places. "We are proud of our heritage. We are proud of who we are, and we have a great deal to be proud of," Velma says.

Mobile serves as a wonderful introduction to this tour of southern cities. After what seems like too brief a stay, you return to the train around mid-afternoon with a stronger sense of southern hospitality and an anticipation for what lies ahead. "As you go through the South, you are going to get the feeling that we are different," says Velma Croom. "We appear to be laid back, but don't let that fool you. We're really with it every minute," she says, smiling.

Leaving Mobile, the train heads briefly north to get around Mobile Bay, providing a few final glimpses of this important body of water and the Alabama state docks, which can handle more than thirty oceangoing vessels at one time. The train again becomes immersed in a watery environment, with broad channels crisscrossing the path of the tracks. Soon you will cross

The AOE *along the Gulf Coast*

over Three Mile Creek on the first of five drawbridges that the tracks pass over in a relatively short distance. After traversing the final drawbridge over the Tensaw River, the train skirts the small Louisiana towns of Bay Minette and Atmore before turning due south toward Pensacola, Florida. At Pensacola, you enjoy your last views of the Gulf of Mexico before the tracks turn sharply east to cut a path across the Florida Panhandle. By the evening, the *American Orient Express* turns north again toward your next destination of Savannah, Georgia. This is one of the longest stretches on board the train and the one night that passengers have dinner and sleep while the train is moving.

This luxury of time allows passengers to relax, settle into the rhythm of the trip, and get to know the train, which will be their home for the next week. On this journey, the train itself is a major focus of the adventure. "It's a beautiful mahogany-paneled train," says Henry Hillman Jr., president and CEO of the American Orient Express Railway Company. On

board to be interviewed for the PBS documentary, he explains that the cars were built in the 1940s and 1950s and are reminiscent of the private cars that people like the Rockefellers and Carnegies owned. More luxuriously appointed than some contemporary trains, the *AOE* features an almost 1920s interior style. Hillman has owned the *AOE* since 1997 and is conta-

giously enthusiastic about long-distance train excursions. "We stop for a full day some places and let you experience both the journey of getting there and the different places we go," he says. "You get close to the things you're passing. You can smell them, you can feel them. You stop at a crossing for another train to go by, and you sit and you feel the desert or the bayou or the swamps." Surrounded by elegance, you have a chance to relive America's golden age of rail travel. "I describe it as a cruise train or a cruise ship on tracks," Hillman says. "It's a relaxing way to see the country."

Plush seating and a circular bay window make the New York Observation Car an elegant place to watch the passing scenery.

AOE *President Henry Hillman Jr.*

One of the railroading traditions that the *American Orient Express* upholds is elegant onboard dining. "Here's your prawn étouffée and here are your medallions of beef with butter beans," says an attentive waiter as he delivers the evening's entrees. "We strive for a sort of casual five-star service," says Henry Hillman. "We want it to be less formal but still top quality."

After dinner, passengers relax in the lounge cars as the train rushes through the night toward Savannah. It is a perfect time for a nightcap or a conversation with new friends. You may also choose to play a board game or relax with a good book. On this trip, the book of choice is the best-selling *Midnight in the Garden of Good and Evil* by John Berendt. "I loved it," says Pam Benson, a passenger from Deerfield, Massachusetts. "It made me want to go to Savannah." Although *Midnight* is primarily the story of an infamous Savannah murder, it also provides an excellent introduction to one of

the South's most fascinating cities. After rumbling through Florida and Georgia during the night, the *AOE* arrives in Savannah in the early morning, before most passengers are awake. After an onboard breakfast, passengers set out for a full day of exploration.

Isolated by forests and tidal flatlands, Savannah is a city steeped in southern traditions and culture. Yet, it was the publication of "The Book," as it is simply known here, that transformed Savannah into a tourist mecca. *Midnight in the Garden of Good and Evil* has brought thousands of people to Savannah and turned author John Berendt into a Savannah icon. "I first came to Savannah in 1982 on a whim," Berendt says. "I had heard about the city. I hadn't seen any pictures of it. I just heard it was very nice. But when I arrived here, I was completely overwhelmed by the beauty of the city. It's a seductively beautiful city."

After deciding that Savannah would be a good subject, Berendt spent seven enjoyable years writing the book. For five of those years, he lived in the city while researching and writing. "I would say the unique element of Savannah is its squares, and those date from the very first days of the colony of Georgia. At every other intersection you have a square . . . . They are absolutely beautiful mini-parks," crows Berendt affectionately. It was in Savannah's Chippewa Square that Tom Hanks waited for a bus in the movie *Forest Gump,*

DINNER ON THE TRAIN

The American Orient Express's executive chef Anthony Hubbard enthusiastically strives to maintain the railroad tradition of fine onboard dining. "They're eating my food three times a day, six days a week," he says. "I like to offer some new foods they haven't had before." Since the AOE operates trips throughout the United States, its menus reflect regional cuisine, and so a distinctive southern flair is apparent in the food offered on this trip. The breakfast menu always includes grits, and for dinner passengers might be served roasted chicken breast with okra corn relish, "dirty" rice, and real southern slaw or seafood étouffée with buttermilk biscuits. As he did at the French Market in New Orleans, Anthony is always on the lookout for local ingredients wherever the train stops. A graduate of the College of Culinary Arts at Johnson and Wales University in Providence, Rhode Island, Anthony has also researched the menus of trains from railroad history, a fact that especially appeals to rail fans. "I incorporate classic train food," Anthony says. "The tarragon-marinated tomato salad with sherry vinaigrette is from the Harvey Houses, which were a famous line of train restaurants. I'm also serving a grilled chicken breast with sweet corn relish that is also classic train fare."

JOHN GRANT

The American Orient Express *upholds the railroad tradition of fine onboard dining.*

Chef Anthony in his onboard kitchen

The luxury rail journey offered by the American Orient Express is enhanced by the dining experience—the quality of the food, the elegant setting, and the excellent service. "There's so many things on the train that we cannot change for the passengers," Anthony says, "such as the limited size of their berthing, the movement of the train, sometimes we have late arrivals and departures. The food is the one thing we can keep consistent and keep them coming back for more." Each evening, Anthony makes a tour of the dining car to introduce himself to passengers and get some firsthand feedback. "It is the best way for me to see how things are going," he says. "A genuine smile is the best compliment I can hope to receive."

Dinner on the train

*Savannah's Historic District, with
its splendid Southern architecture.*

Author John Berendt

but it was Monterey Square that captured Berendt's imagination. By far
Savannah's most notorious square, it was here in the Mercer House in 1981
that a scandalous murder occurred. It shocked the city and became the centerpiece of *Midnight in the Garden of Good and Evil,* which has become an unofficial guide to Savannah. "The thing about *Midnight* and Savannah is that you
can tell in the book how absolutely beautiful the city is," Berendt says. "It
doesn't surprise me that somebody reading the book would want to go to see
Savannah. And of course I'm delighted for Savannah's sake."

Savannah has a remarkable tradition of historic preservation. More than
two thousand restored and preserved buildings and homes make up its

famed Historic District, a two-and-one-half-square-mile area that forms the heart of downtown. One of Savannah's truly special treasures is Bonaventure Cemetery, a place John Berendt calls "one of the most beautiful spots on earth." The evocative cover photo of *Midnight* taken in the cemetery has become a symbol for Savannah. "I had been photographing for a couple nights," says photographer Jack Leigh. "I'd seen all of

One of Savannah's many squares

the statues, I thought, in the cemetery over the years and was astonished to discover this little statue. I think she chose her moment to reveal herself to me." The cover photograph created such enormous interest in the *Bird Girl* statue that, for its own safety, it was moved out of the cemetery to

Savannah's Telfair Museum of Art. "We've had the door flung open by *Midnight* but it's flung open on all these hidden treasures," Leigh says. "When you look around, you see that it is truly layer upon layer of Georgia history. The cemetery really ly hasn't changed since the eigh-

The "Bird Girl" statue at Savannah's Telfair Museum of Art

teenth century, and I think that is what people have really discovered."

The one-day whirlwind tour of Savannah and the Georgia coast leaves most *AOE* passengers wanting more. One of the limitations of this train journey is that its structured itinerary doesn't allow you to decide to spend an extra day or two at a place you discover along the way. The schedule does, however, introduce you to many aspects of the area and offers you an incentive to return. Many people leave Savannah with a promise to come back when they can stay longer.

After a full day of sight-seeing, you return to the *AOE* for dinner and then spend the night on board the train while it is parked on sidetracks near Savannah. The *AOE* gets an early start the following morning, departing Savannah around 7:00 A.M. As most passengers awaken in their sleeping cars, the train crosses the Savannah River and enters South Carolina. Stands of

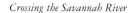

Crossing the Savannah River

joshua, palmetto, and live oak trees line the route, and countless rivers and streams parallel the tracks through the tidal lands of coastal South Carolina. The sun-soaked panorama creates a relaxing setting for passengers enjoying

A cobblestone street in Charleston

a hearty southern breakfast. No matter what else is on the menu, you're sure to be offered some of South Carolina's famed grits, a steamy regional favorite and a great food to jump-start another day of sight-seeing. "In South Carolina," says passenger Willard

Gortner, enjoying the views almost as much as his breakfast, "it wouldn't make a difference what you ordered, you would get grits with it regardless." After breakfast and the short train trip, you leave the train for a daylong tour of another charming southern city.

From a distance, Charleston looks more eighteenth century than twenty-first century, partly because the spires and steeples of more than 180 churches define its skyline. Despite hurricanes, fires, and wars, Charleston has preserved a rich cultural heritage and is one of the nation's most architecturally significant cities. One of the most popular ways to see the architectural diversity of Charleston is on a carriage ride. Tom Doyle has lived in Charleston since 1966 and has been giving horse-drawn carriage tours of

Tom Doyle

the city for more than twenty-five years. "Charleston has over 2,000 buildings that date from the 1800s and earlier," Tom tells his passengers. "This row of buildings is Rainbow Row. Very old. Rainbow Row is pre-Revolutionary." There are few places in the Western Hemisphere where you can see a row of thirteen buildings all more than 200 years old. The sound of horse's hooves echoes off cobblestone streets as the carriage passes the Dock Street Theatre, America's first theater of the performing arts when it opened in 1736. Tom grew up in Connecticut, came south to attend college, met a special girl, and has been sharing Charleston with visitors ever since. "When someone leaves here, they should feel almost like they're a part of Charleston," he says, "and they're going to take a part of it back home with them."

For a glimpse into Charleston's antebellum plantation past, *AOE* passengers visit the Ashley River area. Towering moss-draped oaks have shaded this river for centuries. Before the Civil War, many of South Carolina's most prominent families built plantations along the Ashley River. One of them, Middleton Place, was the home of Arthur Middleton, a signer of the Declaration of Independence. Established in 1741, it includes one of America's oldest landscaped gardens. Visitors have access to about 110 acres of this national historic landmark, and about sixty-five acres of that include a formal garden that has many of the same characteristics as English gardens of the 1700s. The beauty of Middleton Place can lull some to forget that enslaved human beings made

The vibrant colors of Rainbow Row are a reminder that much of Charleston's architectural style is adapted from the West Indies.

The Antebellum plantations along the Ashley River are Charleston's most haunting connection to the past. First laid out in 1741, Middleton Place is considered America's oldest landscaped gardens.

Drayton Hall director Dr. George McDaniel at a low-country oyster roast

southern plantation life possible. It is said that it took one hundred slaves ten years to build the ponds and gardens of Middleton Place. "We don't try to hide the fact that these gardens were developed by slave labor and most of the buildings that exist here were built by slave labor," says Middleton Place museum administrator Tracey Todd. "We try to discuss slavery as accurately as we possibly can. You'll hear interpretations of the lives of enslaved Africans and the types of jobs that they did at Middleton Place." The original mansion was burned to the ground in the waning days of the Civil War. Only a flanker house, now opened as a museum, was salvaged.

Just down the road from Middleton Place is Drayton Hall, one of the most architecturally significant dwellings in America. When Union troops destroyed most of the plantation houses in 1865, Drayton Hall was spared. The reason for its survival remains a mystery. Drayton Hall has been left

JOHN GRANT

completely unfurnished to highlight the original hand-molded plaster ceiling, hand-carved woodwork, and other ornamental details.

Television crews often enjoy opportunities that other visitors miss. On our trip to videotape Drayton Hall, we were invited to join a favorite low-country tradition—a good old-fashioned barbecue and oyster roast. "When you cook a piece of meat and the bone falls out like that, you know you've cooked it right," says Jamie Westendorf, a longtime Charleston caterer. "Ham and carrots, wax beans, fresh green beans, and Vidalia onions, and you're good to go. These are KGB," he says, holding up a bunch of steaming beans, "killer green beans." As with any South Carolina low-country get-together, there's plenty of good food, but the real gustatory draw is the oysters. "This is what used to be done on the plantations years ago," says Drayton Hall director Dr. George McDaniel. "They had outdoor occasions

Drayton Hall

AMERICAN ORIENT EXPRESS PHOTO

The restored cars of the American Orient Express are elegantly appointed with mahogany and brass, exquisite fabrics, and custom carpets.

like this. Family and friends would come by, and oysters were plentiful." McDaniel is shucking oysters for guests at tonight's event. "They roasted them in the shell because that preserves the flavor," he says. "The steam pops them open, then you take this oyster knife and open it up. And then you come in and cut the muscle underneath. Then you put 'em in a little sauce, and they're delicious."

In a day filled with memorable images, the low-country oyster roast provides another intriguing glimpse into southern culture. With all those new experiences and sensations to absorb, it's a good thing that the evening train routine resembles that of the previous day. Passengers return to the *AOE* by early evening in time to relax, have dinner, and enjoy a good night's sleep on the train at the Charleston station.

As the engine rumbles out of Charleston at dawn, passengers ease into another morning on the train. "Good morning! I've got your coffee," says

porter T. J. Jakubic, handing the steaming brew to a pajama-clad passenger in a sleeping car. As another morning on the train gets underway, T. J. and the porters assigned to each sleeping car help organize the awakening travelers. "I basically take care of the passen-

Porter T. J. Jakubic

gers' needs while they're in their sleeping cars," he says. "In the mornings, I do wake-up calls, shower times, and room service. At night, I pull down beds and put out the daily itinerary for the next day so they know what's going on."

Unlike the previous two days, there is no need to hurry through breakfast to meet a tour bus. This is the longest daylight stretch on the train as you make your way across rural South Carolina, through North Carolina, and on to Richmond, Virginia. This extended time on the train allows pas-

sengers a chance to appreciate the pastoral views of the southern countryside and to enjoy the comfort of the train. "The countryside is so glorious,"
says passenger John McLean from San Diego. "You're right in the middle
of it." After two days packed with sight-seeing, this leg of the journey
becomes an enjoyable respite, especially for rail buffs. The passing Carolina
landscape is a patchwork of cotton, tobacco, and soybean fields, and yet
from time to time the route runs right along the original main streets of
many small southern towns.

Railroad historian Brad Lomazzi

Railroad history is the reason Brad Lomazzi is on this train. A railroad
artifact historian, Brad is one of the lecturers the *AOE* takes along
on each of its trips. Along with his
extensive collection of railroad travel
brochures, he shares tales of railroading's past. "In the nineteenth century,
railroads produced tourist guides to
provide additional information to
immigrants and travelers who were all
new to this country," he tells a gathering of passengers in the lounge car.
"Since most passengers were on the
train for adventure, having a travel
guide to learn about the towns they
were going through enabled them to get
more out of their journey. It provided
information about climate, agriculture,
and interesting industry, hunting, and
fishing. All the things that people were
interested in." The printed guides that
Brad shares with passengers draw them
back in time to a different era of
American railroading.

*Old train brochures from
Brad Lomazzi's collection.*

Outside the windows of the *AOE,* another glimpse into days gone
by unfolds as the train leaves North Carolina and crosses high above the
Roanoke River just before entering Virginia in the early afternoon. Nearing
Richmond, the train passes Petersburg, site of one of the longest and

*Crossing the Rantowles Creek
Bridge through rural
South Carolina*

bloodiest battles of the Civil War. The battle for control of this strategic rail center lasted for ten months before the northern forces prevailed. The South surrendered a few weeks later at nearby Appomattox.

Crossing the James River signals the train's arrival at Richmond, Virginia, where passengers will spend the next day and a half. The *AOE* slowly comes to a stop at the historic Union Station, a special treat for rail fans. Amtrak passenger trains no longer stop here since a new station was built in 1975. The *AOE* will remain parked on the tracks behind Union Station for two nights as passengers tour the Richmond area. Talking about Union Station, Walter Witschey, director of the Science Museum of Virginia, says, "This is one of the last great monumental train stations built in the United States before the Depression—a grand piece of Neo-Classical Revival design." At its peak in the 1930s, the Union Station served thousands of passengers a day, but the decline of train travel led the station into disuse. By 1975 the deteriorated building faced demolition, but the citizens of Richmond demanded it be saved.

Where anxious passengers once queued to board the train, curious visitors now explore the world of science. Today the Union Station is home to the Science Museum of Virginia. "It's clear that without a new use and a new vigor such as the Science Museum brings, there would be no money to preserve a building like this and it would be gone," says Witschey. "As we transform it, we end up with a building that is filled each day, and it is that use and activity that are preserving it."

This innovative solution to a fairly typical urban scenario is among the surprises Richmond reveals to most visitors. Few travelers, for instance, are aware that Virginia's state capital is a richly historic city, having played critical roles in southern and American history. During the Revolutionary War, it was the capital of the provisional government and the place where Patrick Henry gave his famous "Give me liberty or give me death" speech. During the Civil War, it was the capital of the

Richmond's Union Station

Confederacy, and its Confederate past is remembered citywide with statues, monuments, and such protected places as Hollywood Cemetery, the final resting place for 18,000 Confederate soldiers. But no place immerses a visitor in the images of the War between the States like the Museum of the Confederacy. Housed here is the world's largest collection of Confederate artifacts—controversial symbols of a time of war, a divided nation, and the Confederacy's defense of slavery.

"This museum is an important stop for anybody who wants to learn more about Richmond's part in the War between the States," says Richard Cheatham, an educator at the museum. "To walk through the galleries of this museum, you're given an almost eerie feeling sometimes when you look at things that surround you. It's awe inspiring to see the actual battle flags that were carried in the field with the bullet holes in them and uniforms with blood stains."

Richard Cheatham

At the State Capitol Building, both the state's Confederate and Revolutionary past are remembered. First occupied in 1788, the magnificent structure was inspired by the designs of Thomas Jefferson and continues to serve as Virginia's seat of government. Its halls are filled with statuary, including the life-sized statue of George Washington, perhaps the most priceless marble statue in the United States.

You'll spend your last night enjoying a farewell dinner on the train as

The AOE *parks behind Richmond's beautifully restored Union Station, now the Science Museum of Virginia.*

it remains parked behind Union Station allowing for time to exchange addresses and memories with newfound friends. The next morning, the final day begins with an early-morning departure from Richmond for the 109-mile, two-hour jaunt north to Washington, D.C. Take a last chance to sit back and enjoy the rural scenery of the rolling hills of Virginia. Outside your windows are the historic town of Fredericksburg and the

Rappahannock River, both quiet landscapes in contrast with the upcoming urban sprawl of northern Virginia and the metro Washington area.

Richmond's Capitol building

Don't let the congestion of this region dampen your spirits too quickly, however. The last few minutes of the trip provide a wonderful short tour of the nation's magnificent capital. The George Washington National Masonic Memorial dominates the skyline as you roll through the suburb of Alexandria, and soon the nation's most treasured monuments come into view. As the train crosses the Potomac, look for the Capitol Dome ahead to the right and the Washington Monument to the left. Surrounded by cherry trees is the Jefferson Memorial, also on the left before the train enters a tunnel that passes under the Capital Mall area. When the train stops, you are in Washington's famed Union Station, ready to debark and perhaps to plan your own long tour of the city's many treasures.

Crossing the Potomac for the final destination, Washington, D.C.

After a week training through the South, you may feel that it no longer seems like a place apart from the rest of America. Like many travelers, however, you may still consider it an enigma. As folklorist Nick Spitzer observed about the South, "We know where it is, but we don't always know how complex and interwoven a culture and landscape it is." The antebellum era between the Revolutionary War and the Civil War looms large as a lasting image leaving visitors much food for thought. We are reminded of the words of Henry Miller: "The old South was plowed under. But the ashes are still warm."

Trip Profile

THE TRAIN:

The trip on the White Pass & Yukon Route Railroad is in comfortable, restored parlor cars, some of which date back to the gold rush period. Each is equipped with a restroom. Every Saturday, the WP&YR also operates a special steam train excursion.

THE ROUTE:

The WP&YR offers two different round-trips: one between Skagway and the White Pass Summit and one between Skagway and Lake Bennett, stopping at the Summit and the town of Fraser.

THE DURATION OF THE TRIP:

The twenty-mile trip to the Summit and back takes about three hours; the forty-mile trip to Lake Bennett takes about eight hours and includes a box lunch.

HIGHLIGHTS:

The train travels along the same path that the gold rush stampeders used late in the 1800s. An onboard guide provides commentary about significant aspects of the train and gold rush history. Skagway, the starting point for the rail journey, is one of the best-preserved Alaskan frontier cities. Visitors can also explore the once thriving, but now abandoned, gold rush sites of Lake Bennett and Dyea.

In July 1897 two steamers docked at busy West Coast ports—the Excelsior *in San Francisco and the* Portland *in Seattle. Few could imagine the impact of the cargo they carried. "The effect of these men coming down the gangplanks loaded with sacks and sacks of gold was electrifying on the whole country," says Karl Gurcke of the National Park Service. "The word got out there was gold in the Klondike, and that really started the stampede. Everybody was heading north."*

ALASKA'S GOLD

GOLD WAS ACTUALLY DISCOVERED NEARLY A YEAR earlier on Rabbit Creek, a small tributary of the Klondike River, by George Washington Carmack and his two Indian companions, Skookum Jim and Dawson Charlie. They decided to work their claim during the winter months and came out of the isolated Yukon Territory when the river thawed the following spring. When they finally arrived in the lower 48, headlines screamed the news: "A Ton of Gold."

RUSH

TRAIN

At that time the United States economy was in a depression following the Panic of 1893, and large segments of the population were destitute. When the Alaskan gold rush stories spread, people scraped together their belongings to head north. Many had only a vague idea of where they were going, but they had clear visions of becoming rich. "They estimate at least a million people were thinking about going to the Klondike," says Gurcke. "A hundred thousand actually left and about thirty to forty thousand staggered into Dawson City about a year or so later."

The gold seekers spent that year just getting to Alaska, climbing over the seemingly impassable mountains and then following a watercourse another five hundred miles before reaching the gold fields. The lure was so strong—bolstered by fantasies of gold nuggets right on the ground—that no obstacle seemed too great. "A lot of them were obsessed about gold," says Gurcke. "It was sort of a mob mentality. You just had to be a little bit faster than the next person."

Bob Doll, general manager of the Alaska Marine Highway System

Shipboard naturalist Rob Morgenthaler

Most stampeders traveled the first leg of the trip by ship through what is known as the Inside Passage to Skagway, Alaska. For the taping of the PBS documentary about the White Pass & Yukon Route Railroad, we retraced part of the journey through the Inside Passage on one of the ferries operated by the Alaska Marine Highway System. "Every year we see a miniature stampede through Alaska. It seems there is always some counterpart to the gold rush occurring," says Bob Doll, general manager of the Alaska Marine Highway System. "It has been oil, it has been fish, and continuing smaller gold efforts. The tourist industry is the latest. Chances are," he says, "the tourist industry will provide the longest running of all of those developments."

The Inside Passage in Southeast Alaska is a place where water and land merge. Giant mountains and glaciers drop right down to the water's edge. "This is a series of drowned mountains," says Bob Doll. "Most people find a corollary in the fjords of Scandinavia and those of New Zealand." The Inside Passage is a protected waterway that runs from Seattle, Washington, to Skagway, Alaska. More than a century ago, it was the quickest way to get to the gold fields. "The Inside Passage really came into its own during the gold rush," notes Rob Morgenthaler, a shipboard naturalist for the U.S. Forest Service. "What's so neat about traveling on the ferries is that we are traveling through the same waterways that a hundred years ago [were used by] the Klondike gold rushers to go to Skagway. The Last Frontier feeling is very much alive and well on the Alaska state ferries."

Most people who arrive in Skagway these days still do so by the water route, coming on giant cruise ships that carry thousands of tourists. On any given day, three or four cruise ships may be docked at Skagway, upholding a tourist tradition as old as the gold rush itself. "The White Pass Railroad has actually been greeting cruise ship passengers since the 1898 Klondike Gold Rush," says Tina Cyr, director of marketing for the White Pass & Yukon Route Railroad. "We had tracks built right down to the waterfront, and they greeted the stampeders and took them up north. Right from the very beginning we had scenic excursions up to Lake Bennett for cruise ship passengers. So today it's very similar," she says. "You're traveling on a 100-year-old train in restored parlor cars, so people really get a sense of what it might have been like for the stampeders."

When the cruise ships dock at Skagway, passengers enter a world that is part living history and part theme park. Dozens of gift shops, small museums, performance halls, and restaurants tell a part of Skagway's gold rush history. Even with the paved

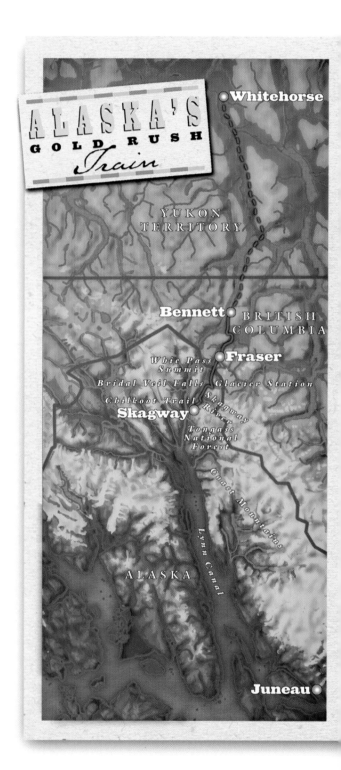

streets clogged with tour buses and
vans, it is easy to let the imagination
drift back more than a century to what
was once a very wild place. "Hello, I'm
Madam Spitfire, an actual madam from
the gold rush days in 1898," says a colorfully dressed woman trying to entice
passersby on a tour of the Red Onion
Saloon. "The Red Onion was a very fancy brothel in the gold rush days,"
she says. "It would cost a gentleman five dollars to come upstairs." Today,
for about the same price, Madam Spitfire takes you upstairs for a history
lesson. "The Red Onion had ten rooms holding the fanciest, most beautiful
women in Skagway. It was a very exciting time."

Madam Spitfire

The Red Onion Saloon is just one of many original gold rush buildings
in Skagway. The Klondike Gold Rush National Historical Park is a unique
preservation partnership of the town, local businesses, and the federal government. "The park is comprised of fifteen historical buildings, eight of
those leased by private owners and used as private businesses in town," says
Linda Cook of the National Park Service. "Visitors have the benefit of
walking back in time," Linda says. "The same path that those tens of thousands of gold seekers came a hundred years ago."

During the summer months, Skagway is a very busy place, with close
to 900,000 visitors. Skagway's permanent population of around 800 people
more than doubles with seasonal workers during the tourist season, and

*Preserved buildings within the
Klondike Gold Rush National
Historical Park*

nearly every one of them has a cruise ship schedule handy.
In fact, just about everything in town is geared to the
cruise ships' schedules. Restaurants and shops even set
their hours to coincide with the ships' arrivals and departures. During the busiest periods, Skagway buzzes with
the sound of helicopters, train whistles, buses, vans, horse-
drawn carriages, and other tour operations. The evenings
and weekends are a much quieter time in Skagway, and the
sense of the past is even more alive. Very early in the morning is an especially pleasant time to walk the streets of Skagway, stopping in at the
Sweet Tooth Cafe for friendly service, good coffee, and a sweet roll.

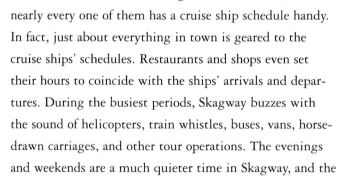

"Every morning we re-create the Klondike Gold Rush all over again," says Steve Hites, a local businessman and entertainer who enthusiastically combines those talents during his Skagway Streetcar tours. "Eight blocks of bliss laid out for your entertainment," Steve tells a carful of tourists. "On the left, covered with 10,000 pieces of driftwood, is the Arctic Brotherhood Hall. This was a social club during the gold rush. Today it's our city museum." The long yellow "streetcars" used for the tours have become a Skagway landmark. The distinctive vehicles were once used for tours in Yellowstone, Yosemite, and other national parks. "The Mascot Saloon [was] one of seventy-five watering holes in Skagway at the height of the gold rush. You would have been tripping over saloons walking down the street," Steve recounts for a carload of wide-eyed visitors. "You cannot buy a beer in there, but the National Park Service will interpret for you what a beer would have tasted like," he says, smiling.

The Golden North Hotel in Skagway has been operating continuously since the gold rush days.

Streetcar tour guide Steve Hites

*Some 800,000 visitors a year crowd
the streets of tiny Skagway.*

As visitors explore Skagway, the sound of trains is ever present. The tracks cross Broadway, and trains are in constant motion between the docks, the depot, and the trip up the mountain. Every Tuesday, Wednesday, and Thursday—the days when the most cruise ships are in town—the WP&YR operates four trains in the morning and another four in the afternoon. Three trains make the round-trip between Skagway and the White Pass Summit in about three hours. One train each morning and afternoon continues on to Fraser and then Lake Bennett, making the round-trip in about eight hours. The Lake Bennett trip includes a box lunch provided by the railroad. On busy days in the summer, the railroad adds an evening Summit train, a special treat since Alaska's nearly endless summer days provide different shades of light and new perspectives on the route. Friday through Monday, the WP&YR operates two trains in the morning and two in the afternoon, one each to the Summit and Lake Bennett.

During the peak hours in the early morning and early afternoon, as many as four trains depart in a very short span of time. The station bustles with energy and anticipation, but there is very little confusion. The courteous railroad staff guides passengers to

Tina Cyr

the right train and the correct car. Certain cars are designated for tour groups, heli-hikers, those continuing on to Bennett, and independent passengers. You will enjoy the ride in one of the parlor cars, some of which are more than one hundred years old. "The oldest is the Lake Emerald, car 244," says Tina Cyr. "It's older than the railroad itself, built in 1883." The cars are all beautifully restored to reflect the gold rush era. The work on the cars, as well as the maintenance on the engines, is done in the train shops by a dedicated staff of engineers and craftsmen.

The trip taken by today's tourist is on the same route used by trains that took the stampeders north, although today's trip is much shorter than the original route. "Originally, the White Pass Railroad was 110 miles—Skagway, Alaska, to Whitehorse, Yukon. That was where the stampeders floated down the Yukon River to get to the Dawson gold mines," Tina Cyr

The WP&YR operates fifty-one passenger cars. The oldest is the Lake Emerald. Built in 1883, it predates the railroad.

says. "We operate forty miles of the original 110-mile line now." Tracks still run the full length of the route, and the WP&YR is working on upgrading the rails farther north and may decide to extend the longer trip as far as Carcross at milepost 67. Since most visitors who come off the cruise ships have a limited amount of time, however, they take the shorter Summit round-trip. This means there is little economic incentive to operate an excursion train along the full original route.

Even on this abbreviated excursion, a great sense of adventure and anticipation is apparent among the passengers as the train pulls out of Skagway. It is impossible not to imagine what it must have been like to be on this train more than a hundred years ago. "Welcome aboard the White Pass and Yukon Railroad," says Kori Goertz, the train guide who will share insights with passengers throughout the trip. "We are truly going to be following along the footsteps of history this afternoon." The WP&YR provides passengers with its *All Aboard* magazine, which includes an excellent route map listing all important spots on the route. Milepost markers are easy to read on the side of the tracks, so passengers can easily enjoy a self-guided adventure right from their seats. Several good books and pamphlets about the history of the railroad and the gold rush are also on sale at the depot.

Kori Goertz

The Gold Rush Cemetery

Shortly after leaving the station, the train passes through the outskirts of Skagway and goes by the WP&YR train shops where the railroad repairs and maintains its equipment. Just past the shops, the train slows to give passengers a good look at the Gold Rush Cemetery where many stampeders are buried. Skagway's most notorious citizen lies there among them. "Soapy Smith was a con man. He was undoubtedly one of the smoothest operators in American western history," says Steve Hites. "At the height of his power, Soapy controlled the entire town." Although Smith was the grand marshal of the Fourth of July parade and did much to help develop Skagway, he ultimately became a menace who threatened the prosperity of the town. A

By the time the White Pass & Yukon Route was completed, the gold rush was nearly over. However, the WP&YR has enjoyed a rich and colorful history hauling freight and passengers.

FIRST EXCURSION TRAIN IN ALASKA
SKAGUAY, JULY 21, 1898

WP&YR COLLECTION

frustrated business community met on July 8, 1898, to decide how to deal with Smith. "Soapy's been drinking all day. That night, grabbing his Winchester, he goes down to the dock," says Hites. "Guarding the dock is Frank Reid, the city engineer." What happens next is Skagway's tallest tale and an illuminating insight into the Wild West atmosphere of the time. "Reid and Soapy are about ten paces apart. Both men fire simultaneously. Smith takes a bullet in the heart and is dead before he hits the dock," continues Hites. "Frank Reid takes a bullet in the groin, shattering his pelvis, and dies twelve agonizing days later." The grateful community built a large monument to Reid in the cemetery that reads, HE GAVE HIS LIFE FOR THE HONOR OF SKAGWAY. Smith is buried at the edge of the cemetery. "Over the years," says Hites, "Soapy, of course, is the one that the pathway is beaten to at the edge of the Gold Rush Cemetery."

Just past the cemetery, the train crosses Reid Creek and soon reaches its top speed of twenty-five miles per hour. A few miles farther north, the train crosses the East Fork of the Skagway River at Denver and begins its ascent. A popular three-and-a-half-mile hiking trail leads from the tracks to Denver Glacier, some 2,500 feet higher in elevation. A refurbished WP&YR caboose parked at the trailhead is used by weary hikers and can be rented for overnight stays through the U.S. Forest Service. As the train crosses the Denver Glacier Bridge, you'll have an excellent opportunity to photograph all of the parlor cars and the two engines stretched along the curve.

Wary passengers glance down at the canyon below.

The train continues to climb, passing a clearing in the trees that provides a panoramic view back down to Skagway and the Lynn Canal, some seven miles below. After crossing three small bridges, the train enters a granite corridor along the narrowest part of the canyon. Rocky cliffs hover on one side, and the steep river canyon is on the other. This is the first area where heavy rock had to be blasted so that the rail bed could be built. As the train wraps around the mountain on a shelf of granite blasted out of the cliff, you begin to understand why this route is considered such an engineering and construction accomplishment.

Across the canyon to the left, you can see the Klondike Highway and the U.S. Customs station. The Customs station is located twelve miles south of the actual border because of the fierce winds and blizzards that frequently occur on the international line. Considered something special in these parts, the highway makes Skagway one of only three towns in all of Southeast Alaska accessible by road.

High above the tracks, Goat Lake feeds a giant patchwork waterfall that cascades about 1,800 feet down the mountain and passes under the tracks. Pitchfork Falls gets its name from the way the main waterfall splits into several forks below the tracks. The train slows so passengers get a good look as the water rushes down the mountain and beneath the tracks. Be on the lookout—it passes very quickly. You can't see the pitchfork pattern from the train, but it is easily seen from the highway on the other side of the canyon.

Just a little farther up the tracks is one of the most solemn spots on the route. "This brings us to milepost 10.4—Black Cross Rock," Kori informs the passengers. "Off the left side of the train is a clearing about a hundred feet below.

You'll see a huge hundred-ton granite slab that came crashing down the mountainside during a blasting accident, instantly crushing two railroad workers." A small black wooden cross marks the site as a memorial to the more than thirty men who lost their lives building the railroad.

As the train passes the halfway point to the Summit, another spectacular waterway comes into view. Across the canyon is Bridal Veil Falls. This time the train offers the perfect perspective to see it in its entirety. As many as twenty-two channels can be seen during the peak runoff period in the spring-time, but even in summer it is an impressive sight as it tumbles 6,000 feet down the far mountainside. The train slows to allow passengers to see the cascade through an opening in the treeline.

Not much farther along, the train breaks away from the original White Pass Trail as it enters what is called the "highline" section of the route. The train makes a three-mile horseshoe loop to gain elevation along one of the steepest narrow-gauge rail lines in America. "Narrow-gauge tracks are laid just three feet apart," explains Kori. "Standard gauge rails are four feet, eight and one-half inches apart." The narrow-gauge tracks require less space for the rail bed and are better able to negotiate the tight curves along the route.

Beyond the round-trip train journey, some visitors want to explore more of the Alaskan wilderness, and the White Pass & Yukon Route is a good starting point for such made-to-order adventure. Glacier Station at milepost 14 is a flag stop for the WP&YR and the starting point for a trail to Laughton Glacier. The train drops off and picks up passengers who want to take day hikes or even

stay overnight at a Forest Service cabin. You just need to check with the ticket office to make the arrangements. The mile-and-a-half hike is through the rain forest of the Tongas National Forest, with great views of the Sawtooth Range, the raging Skagway River, and Laughton Glacier. One especially dramatic way to see more of Alaska is a combination rail/air/hiking tour. Packer Expeditions provides heli-hiking tours that

The WP&YR's narrow-gauge tracks are essential for negotiating the tight curves of this mountain ter-rain.

The WP&YR drops off and picks up passengers at several hiking trails along the route to the summit.

Carl Mulvihill

include a helicopter excursion of the area and a landing right next to the tracks at Glacier Station. You then hike to the glacier before returning to board a special car on the southbound train. The hike is not difficult, and the combination of the flight, the

hike, and the train is a sensational way to explore this majestic region.

Railroad workers would hang from ropes to drill holes and plant black powder to clear away the rock.

Immediately after passing Glacier Station, the train glides over a steel bridge that crosses a major fork of the Skagway River. Terrific views of the cascading water captivate passengers on both sides of the train. As the train slowly crosses the bridge, it makes a complete horseshoe, providing views of all of the cars strung out on the curve. Soon the train begins a steady climb through the steepest part of the route. Slippery Rock is a bare, very steep area that required workers to drill blasting holes by hand into the solid rock. Carl Mulvihill, unofficial historian for the WP&YR, talks about the construction of the road bed: "The hardest part was the actual drilling. They [were] working on a cliff, hanging from ropes. It was quite dangerous. It took them two years to build the railroad. Everything that was used—the ties, the rails, the rolling stock, dynamite, people—all had to be brought up here by barge or ship." Mulvihill, like many here, has long ties to the gold rush railroad. "My grandfather came here in 1900 as a train dispatcher. My father worked for the railroad for about forty years until

H.C. BARLEY COLLECTION

he retired, and I've put in seventeen years in the railroad," he says with obvious pride. "We get a lot of people who have traveled around the world, and they describe this as the prettiest portion of all of their world travels."

As the bald top of Slippery Rock disappears from view, the train climbs through a perfectly U-shaped valley that was carved by the glaciers during the Ice Age. During wildflower season, the side of the tracks is alive with color. Red elderberry bushes are everywhere. Their clusters of red berries are toxic if eaten raw, but they make great wine, jam, and jelly when cooked. Fireweed, a very pretty magenta-colored flower, is also prevalent along the route. Common in the Yukon Territory and other parts of Alaska, it is so named because it is the first flower to grow back after a fire. "You're going to want to have your cameras ready as we're coming up to one of the most spectacular portions of our trip," announces Kori. "We're going to cross over Glacier Gorge, a thousand feet above the valley floor. Those who are a little wary of heights might not want to peer off to the left," Kori cautions. "This is going to look like we're floating a thousand feet above the valley on a wooden trestle constructed back in 1898." The sensation is breathtaking as you glance over the edge of the train and see nothing but the rocky valley below.

Immediately after crossing the bridge, you are startled again as the train is blanketed in darkness as it enters the first of two tunnels on the route. The only tunnel required on the original route, this and the wooden trestle were both constructed during the harshest winter months of 1898. Kori reports that the tunnel workers needed three months to drill the 600 feet through the mountain. After passing through the tunnel, the train climbs past Inspiration Point, where passengers look back for another incredible view of the Inside Passage and Skagway sitting serenely seventeen miles below.

The peaceful journey through this magnificent scenery doesn't reveal that this area was the site of some of the darkest moments of the gold rush. "The White Pass became known as the Dead Horse Trail because of the thousands of horses that died along the trail," says National Park Service historian Karl Gurcke. "They were so obsessed for the gold they abused the horses." When the railroad to the Summit was completed in February 1899, the horse trail was abandoned. Remains of the old gold rush tent

ENGINE 73

Once a week during the summer, the White Pass & Yukon Route offers a truly unique rail experience. "We have the last operating steam locomotive in the United

States for a narrow-gauge train," says Gary Danielson, vice president of marketing. "Every Saturday throughout the summer we run a special steam excursion from Skagway up to Lake Bennett." The round-trip takes about eight hours, and the train stops several times to give passengers a chance to photograph the steam engine. "On the days when the steam engine runs, the real rail fans come out. They sort of plan their trip to Skagway for this event. People have come from all over the world to ride our train," Danielson says. "The steam train coupled with the scenery usually brings a lot of 'oohs and ahs.' People really feel they've had a different experience."

Engine No. 73 was built by the Baldwin Locomotive Works in 1947, and it was the last steam narrow-gauge engine built in the United States. The spectacular steam journey offered by the WP&YR only hints at the colorful history of this engine. "It was in service until 1963 when it was replaced by diesel engines. It was put on display up at Lake Bennett for many years and frankly forgotten," says Danielson. "In the early 1980s it was restored by our rail shops people and then put into service. It takes a lot of babying, a lot of maintenance. In fact, that's why

Engine No. 73 was built by the Baldwin Locomotive Works in 1947, and it was the last narrow-gauge steam engine built in the United States.

steam engines were eventually phased out across North America—because of the amount of maintenance and work it takes to keep them up."

Another highlight for rail fans is parked just outside the train station next to the main street. "Our rotary snowplow is unique because there are only two like it in North America—a steam-driven, narrow-gauge, rotary snowplow," says Tina Cyr. "It was what made our railroad able to operate for the first sixty years, to be able to clear the line in the pass." The WP&YR operates the snowplow each spring to clear the last snow from the tracks before the trains begin to run. Although no longer essential to the railroad's operation, it remains another connection to the rail line's past. "It's a beautiful hunk of machinery," Tina says, revealing a true railroader's awe and respect for this little gem of history.

The powerful rotary snowplow's whirling ten-foot blades chew into snow drifts each spring to help clear the rails. Built in 1898, it is one of just two steam-driven narrow-gauge rotary snowplows still operating in North America.

city and the white bones of horses lie throughout the area, which is part of the Klondike Gold Rush National Historical Park.

As the train nears the Summit, it arrives at another of the engineering marvels of the route—a giant steel cantilever bridge that sits off to the left. At the time of its construction in 1901, it was the tallest railroad bridge of its kind in the world. It stands 215 feet above Dead Horse Gulch. The old bridge was used for sixty-eight years before being replaced in 1969 when the railroad began carrying heavier loads of lead, zinc, and silver. Along with the new bridge, a new tunnel was blasted through the mountain to facilitate the climb to the Summit.

As the train pulls away from the second tunnel and curves around the solid rock face of the mountain, you can get a glimpse of the actual White Pass Trail—a thin path through the rocks marked by a small sign below the tracks that reads TRAIL OF '98. Only a few feet wide, the path

JOHN GRANT

The wooden trestle and tunnel at Glacier Gorge were constructed during the harshest winter months of 1898. The trestle stands a thousand feet above the valley.

182

 provides the most visible image of what stampeders faced as they made their way north. During the television production trip, the WP&YR arranged for the PBS crew to take a work train up to this area around six o'clock one morning so we could be in position to get a shot of the train as it passed a few hours later. On that typically misty morning, we had time to climb down the rocky ledge from the tracks and cross over to the trail. It was a haunting experience to peer through the fog at the narrow path that more than a hundred years ago was the gateway for tens of thousands of men and women seeking fame and fortune.

Leaving behind the ghostly images evoked by the sight of the trail, the passengers on the gold rush train are soon brought back to the present. Only a mile from the pathway, the train reaches the White Pass Summit at

an elevation of 2,865 feet. Two flags fly to the west on a high mound to mark the boundary between the United States and Canada. Most of the WP&YR trains pull onto a 1,650-foot siding at the Summit. The engines are moved from one end of the train to the other, passengers flip their seat backs to face the opposite way, and soon the train heads south down the mountain for the return trip to Skagway. Luckily, our train adventure isn't over, however. We have plans to continue on to Fraser to change trains for the trip to historic Lake Bennett.

Continuing on an upward climb, the train quickly passes through Meadows, a reference point for dispatchers. Actually the highest point on the rail line, it is some seventy-five feet higher than the Summit. Stands of alpine firs and pine trees dot the landscape as the train enters an area of larger ponds and lakes. For miles and miles, the landscape takes on an otherworldly look, a delightful variation from the earlier part of the trip.

Less than thirty minutes after passing the Summit, the train arrives at Fraser, a water stop for the steam trains

The southbound train crosses a glacial river between Fraser and the White Pass Summit.

of another era. Its old red two-story water tank building remains, and is the last such structure on the rail line. Today Fraser is a major transfer point for the White Pass & Yukon Route Railroad. Many of the folks who arrived in Skagway by cruise ship leave the train here to board buses to explore other areas of Alaska and Canada before returning to their ships.

Fraser Station was once an important water stop for steam engines.

Diehard rail fans and more independent travelers, on the other hand, simply change trains here for the added adventure that awaits on the journey to Bennett. Since fewer people make this longer excursion, the WP&YR uses smaller trains to make the trip.

Although the trip from Fraser to Bennett is only twelve miles, it takes nearly an hour. Once again the landscape changes as the train winds its way along the shore of Summit Lake. While the train traces the bend of the lake around a rock bluff known as Ptarmigan Point, conductor John McDermott greets his passengers: "Welcome aboard the Lake Bennett Adventure Rail Excursion," he says. "We're going along the area of the White Pass Trail as it crossed the Summit and went down into Lake Bennett." John started with the WP&YR in 1972 and, like so many people in Alaska, has a great story to tell. "My wife and I live in the last standing building left from the gold rush in the old town of Dyea," he tells his passengers. "Back in 1976 we bought a log cabin, fourteen by eighteen feet." John regales the passengers with tales of outhouse adventures, pesky bears, and the joys and tribulations of living in the Alaskan wilderness. "They

John McDermott, the singing conductor

finally came out with these meter-sized [satellite] dishes that work out here, and now I get sixty channels. The winters go by an awful lot better."

At Log Cabin, a major tent city on the White Pass Trail during the gold rush, the train crosses the South Klondike Highway and heads deep into the wilderness, begin-

Bennett Station

JOHN GRANT

Surrounded by cloud-topped mountains, Lake Bennett, British Columbia, is a serene setting and an ideal place to end the rail journey on Alaska's Gold Rush Train.

ning a slow descent into Bennett. Beaver Lake is the first of several large bodies of water you pass along this section of the route. Next is Lake Lindeman, which was one of the areas where stampeders stopped to build their boats for the rest of the journey to the gold fields. At the end of the descent, the train rounds a curve and you can see Bennett Station and Lake Bennett just ahead. The view south down the lake is awe-inspiring. Surrounded by cloud-topped mountains, it is a serene setting, an image in sharp contrast to the wild times of the gold rush period. Passengers on the WP&YR have two hours to explore the old station, wander through the remnants of the gold rush tent city that once dominated this area, and take in the peace and tranquility of one of the most beautiful spots along the path to the gold fields.

For generations the Chilkat Indians used the Chilkoot Pass and Lake Bennett to reach the interior of the Yukon. Early Europeans used the same route in the early 1880s in search of gold. It wasn't until the gold strike in 1897 that madness prevailed. "Bennett is located at the end of the Chilkoot and White Pass Trails, so during the gold rush this would have been a

boat-building center," says Rob Scoble, an interpreter for Parks Canada, who oversees the site and provides guided tours of the area. "The time when Bennett would have had its maximum population would have been just before the ice went out in the

Rob Scoble

spring of '98. At that time, there were likely close to 20,000 people in Bennett," he says. "When the ice finally did go out, about 7,000 boats headed down Lake Bennett for Dawson City."

Bennett is an ideal place to end this gold rush rail adventure. It is a quiet, peaceful setting where the sense of the gold rush is everywhere. "The historical footprint of the old town is used to define the campground," says Scoble about the campground for hikers operated by Parks Canada at the site of what was once the tent city of Bennett. "You can walk along the main street, which is the main pathway that goes through the campground, and you can see piles of artifacts that are associated with different business-es." Piles of old rusted cans mark the Bennett Bakery. Near the collections

TWO TRAILS TO GOLD

At the end of the Inside Passage, stampeders found the small Alaskan frontier towns of Skagway and Dyea, neither prepared to handle the crush of new arrivals. "It was a madhouse. It was crazy," says Karl Gurcke, who studies Skagway and Dyea as part of his work with the National Park Service. In

1897 only a few hundred people lived in both towns. With the arrival of the stampeders, the towns grew to tens of thousands almost overnight. "The intent was to get over the mountains down to Dawson and there were two trails leading over the mountains," Gurcke says—"the White Pass Trail leading out of Skagway and the Chilkoot Trail leading out of Dyea." The Chilkoot was more popular with the early gold rush crowd. It was shorter but had a very steep pass at the summit. The White Pass was a longer but more gradual ascent. "Take your pick," says Gurcke. "They were both horrendous."

When the railroad picked the White Pass as the only possible rail route over the mountains, the Chilkoot Trail and Dyea were abandoned. "By 1902 the post office closed, and there were less than half a dozen people in Dyea," says Gurcke. Today the National Park Service owns most of the land in Dyea, and Gurcke spends time trying to reconstruct its history. "Dyea is a symbol of the gold rush. It's a town that didn't survive. Skagway survived; Dyea didn't," he says. "It's important because it says something about ourselves, about the human species, about the transience of our existence and what we build."

The legacy of Dyea and the Chilkoot Trail remains alive along the actual hiking trail that is jointly maintained by the United States and Canada. The trail is thirty-four

The last standing storefront in Dyea

Karl Gurcke

miles from Dyea to Lake Bennett and welcomes more than 3,500 hikers a year. Most people take three to five days to complete the hike. "It enables the hiker to get a little bit of understanding of what it was like in the gold rush days," says Tim Steidel, the National Park Service lead ranger for the Chilkoot Trail. "The artifacts are still there along the trail, only they've been hidden in dense brush," he says. "We put exhibits and interpretations along the trail at all the major historic town sites to help bring the past alive a little bit." Even though today's hikers have much better gear and don't need to carry the 2,000 pounds of supplies hauled in by most stampeders, the strenuous Chilkoot Trail isn't for everyone. "The physical challenge that is required getting over the Chilkoot Trail is very real," Steidel says, "but it's pretty incredible."

Chilkoot Trail Unit
Klondike Gold Rush National Historical Park

of broken bottles and piles of glass are the sites of the many hotels that sold liquor. These unusual "exhibits" have a purpose that Scoble soon reveals. "It helps people engage their imaginations a little bit, because that's ultimately what you have to do to understand the gold rush," he says.

Hikers at Bennett Station

When the White Pass & Yukon Route Railroad connected Skagway and Whitehorse, Bennett quickly became a ghost town, no longer needed as a stopover on the way to the gold fields. "It would have pretty much disappeared overnight," Scoble says. The only structure left standing at the site is St. Andrew's Presbyterian Church. "It's become a bit of a symbol of the gold rush because it is the only standing structure that dates back to the gold rush era. One of the interesting things about it is that the siding on the church is actually quarter rounds that were sliced off the railway ties that were used for the White Pass Railway."

The WP&YR itself serves a different purpose than it did a hundred years ago at Bennett. Today it brings visitors to one of the more isolated areas of the gold rush, and it ferries hikers coming off the Chilkoot Trail back to civilization. Wisely, the railroad provides a separate car for the weary—and often in need of a bath—hikers after their strenuous trip, which usually takes three to five days to complete.

For tourists and hikers alike, the southbound trip back to Skagway on the White Pass & Yukon Route is a time to reflect on the beauty of the rail journey and the romance of the gold rush. "One thing that is kind of interesting about my job," says National Park Service historian Karl Gurcke, "is that I meet the descendants of many of these individuals—people whose father or mother or grandfather went on the stampede. And the stories come down that it was this extraordinary, wonderful, exciting adventure." Learning more about this event that occurred more than a hundred years ago makes us reflect on ourselves, Gurcke says. "Would we go on a gold rush? Would we be taken out by this mass stampede?" he asks. It is an interesting question to ponder as you gaze out on the remnants of one of the most colorful episodes in American history.

Appendix

How to Book Your Own
Great American Rail Journey

The Alaska Railroad

P.O. Box 107500

Anchorage, AK 99510

Reservations: (800) 544–0552

Email: reservations@akrr.com

Website: www.akrr.com

The Copper Canyon

Sierra Madre Express

P.O. Box 26381

Tucson, AZ 85726

Reservations: (800) 666–0346 or (520) 747–0346

Email: adventure@sierramadreexpress.com

Website: www.sierramadreexpress.com

Or contact

Tauck Tours, Inc.

P.O. Box 5027

Westport, CT 06881

(800) 468–2825

The American South by Rail and The Rockies by Rail

American Orient Express

5100 Main Street

Suite 350

Downers Grove, IL 60515

Reservations: (800) 320–4206 (between 8:30 A.M. and 6:00 P.M. CST)

For brochure: (877) 854–3545

The Coast Starlight and The Adirondack

Amtrak

(800) USA–RAIL

Website: www.amtrak.com

The Skeena

Via Rail Canada

1150 Station Street

Vancouver, BC

Canada, V6A 2X7

Reservations: (800) 561–8630

Website: www.viarail.ca

Alaska's Gold Rush Train

White Pass & Yukon Route

P.O. Box 435, Dept. B

Skagway, AK 99840

(800) 343–7373 or (907) 983–2217

Fax: (907) 983–2734

Email: info@whitepass.net

Website: www.whitepassrailroad.co

Index

About the Author

JOHN GRANT IS PRESIDENT AND EXECUTIVE PRODUCER OF

Driftwood Productions, Inc. He has created and executive produced nine

train programs for public television distribution, several episodes of which

he also produced or coproduced. He created and executive-produced the

PBS television series *Legendary*

Lighthouses; co-authored, along with

Ray Jones, the companion book for

that series; and produced the *Staying*

at a Lighthouse special for PBS. Prior

to creating Driftwood Productions,

Grant was senior vice president of

national programming at the Public

Broadcasting Service (PBS) in Alexandria, Virginia, from 1990 to 1995. He

also spent sixteen years at WPSX-TV, the public television station at Penn

State University.

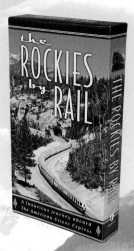

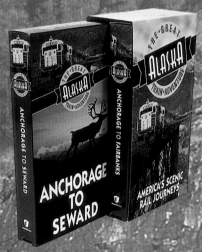
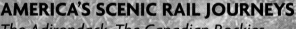

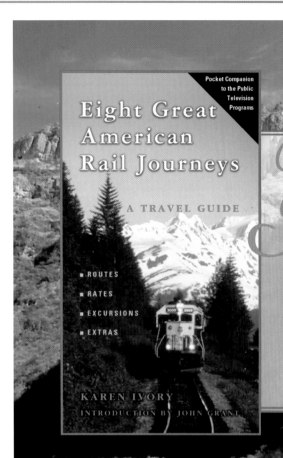

Eight Great American Rail Journeys

A TRAVEL GUIDE

Pocket Companion to the Public Television Programs

■ ROUTES
■ RATES
■ EXCURSIONS
■ EXTRAS

KAREN IVORY

INTRODUCTION BY JOHN GRANT

*You've read the book...
Now live the dream!*

Plan your own great rail journey with this full-color pocket companion travel guide to some of America's most scenic and historically rich landscapes. It provides everything you need to know to get on board and make the journey of a lifetime! Each chapter profiles one trip, including a short synopsis of the trip, rate information, food served on board, side excursion information, transportation, accommodations, and more.

Also by John Grant ▶

Few historic structures are more beautiful, venerable, or romantic than lighthouses. As seen on PBS, this official companion celebrates America's rich lighthouse heritage by exploring six distinct coastal regions and visiting the extraordinary lighthouses that serve them. Lavishly illustrated, it showcases dozens of delightful characters, tells dramatic stories of heroism and tragedy, and evokes everything we love about these grand watchmen.

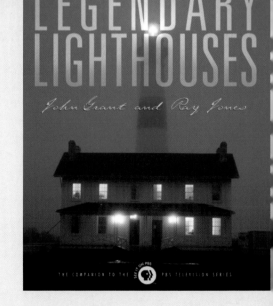

LEGENDARY LIGHTHOUSES

John Grant and Ray Jones

THE COMPANION TO THE PBS TELEVISION SERIES

The Globe Pequot Press

To order, contact your local bookstore or call 800–243–0495 • *www.globe-pequot.com*